*The Search for
Prosperity*

The Search for Prosperity

Emigration from Britain

1815–1930

Richard Garrett

"We have frequently heard the character of emigrant
ships from Ireland declared to be worse than that
of those concerned in the slave trade of Africa."
(Montreal Advertiser, 1834.)

"The miserable hath no other medicine
But only hope."
(William Shakespeare, *Measure for Measure*.)

WAYLAND PUBLISHERS LONDON

IN THIS SERIES:
English Life in the Seventeenth Century
English Life in the Eighteenth Century
English Life in the Nineteenth Century
English Life in Tudor Times
English Life in Chaucer's Day
Roger Hart

FORTHCOMING
The English Aristocracy Marion Yass
The Cost of Living in Britain
Leith McGrandle
Immigration to Britain Colin Nicolson
The Growth of Literacy Christine Wiener

Contents

1 *The Human Scrap Heap*

THE ARRIVAL OF A NEW CENTURY is as good an occasion as any for letting off fireworks: for making new resolutions and for finding reasons for fresh hopes. The nineteenth century was heralded with as much optimism as any other. There were pious, if jingoistic, affirmations of a will to "stride forward into a new epoch with proud hearts and heads held high" – and all that. In fact, for many people, the new epoch which had come without invitation was a cheat.

King George III more than amply occupied the throne, secure in the knowledge that only God and he knew the answers. In 1760, the population of Britain had been seven or eight million. By 1820, it had become fifteen million. It may not seem to be very many by today's standards, but it meant that a great many extra mouths had to be fed. Too many. It also meant that there were many more bodies to be clad. Again: too many. In spite of the ingenuity of the inventors, there were not enough clothes. Nor, in a great many cases, was there sufficient money with which to buy them.

Agricultural and Industrial Revolutions

Both problems were being, in a manner of speaking, grappled with. For the moment, however, the cure was worse than the disease. In the world of farming, enclosure – the main feature of the Agricultural Revolution – had begun. The country was being carved up into a pattern of neat, rectangular fields, each surrounded by a hedgerow. Acres of woodland were being cut down to clear a way for the plough: a sensible system of rotating the crops was being introduced. It all suggested progress. There seemed every reason to believe that a determined, even scientific, effort was being made to feed those extra mouths, and this was no doubt true. The trouble was that, in this new agricultural picture, there was little place for the peasant. His smallholding had no part in the grand design: it had to be erased.

The situation, for the ambitious farmer, was excellent. In many instances, he had more land than ever before, and there was certainly no shortage of labour. The little men, who were being evicted from their holdings, could either work for him – or get out. With so much help available, wages became lower and lower until, for there seems to be no limit to human cupidity, they were barely enough to keep a family alive.

Nor were the cities doing very much to help. With the invention of the steam engine, man had discovered a new toy. It offered superb possi-

Opposite. Emigration was the last resort of the poor, the dispossessed and the hungry.

A pretty view, but enclosures of the fields made thousands jobless in early nineteenth-century Britain.

bilities for transportation. It also pointed the way to mass production and unemployment. The Luddites may have been trying to halt the tide of progress when they wrought their damage on factories in the Midlands, but they knew what they were about. The steam jenny alone added steeply to the number who were out-of-work. Frameworkers, in particular, suddenly found themselves without jobs and uncertain of where to go. What is more, the great concentrations of mills and workshops in the towns virtually put an end to the cottage industries. The peasant's wife, who had been gainfully busy with such pursuits as spinning and knitting, discovered that nobody wanted her products any more. They could be manufactured in much greater quantities, and far more cheaply, with the help of a steam engine. Her plight was not unlike that of her husband : the pile of human scrap was beginning to grow.

After the Napoleonic Wars

The end of the Napoleonic Wars in 1815 made the situation even worse. About half-a-million ex-soldiers suddenly came on to the labour market; industry, which had enjoyed an artificial wartime boom, sighed into a depression; and bad harvests from 1816 to 1818 caused the farmers to prune their payrolls still more. In many parts of the country, conditions were appalling. Nor did they show any signs of recovering. In 1828, a man named Lister, who lived at Minster in Kent, told a House of

Commons committee which had been formed to investigate property that: "The convicts on board the hulks are a great deal better off than our labouring poor, let the convict be ever so bad a man. The convicts come on shore to work; they do not work so hard nor so many hours as the common labourers, and they live better. It is very common for the convicts to save money, and to carry from £10 to £40 away from the hulks when they are discharged."

Henry Boyce, who also lived in Kent, had this to say: "I have seen 30 or 40 young men, in the prime of life, degraded by being hooked on to carts and wheelbarrows, dragging stones to the highways, because they could get no employment elsewhere. In the parish of Ash, there is a regular meeting every Thursday, where the paupers are put up for auction and their labour sold for a week, and it often happens that there is no bidder."

A magistrate from Wiltshire had no better news. He told the committee: "According to the price of labour . . . the weekly earning of a man, wife, and one son, amount to nine shillings; and if a man has five children besides, he is allowed, in relief, 1s. 9½d. [9p.] a week in addition to the earnings. As the price of bread is 1s. 3d. [6p.] for a gallon-loaf, each of these people has 160 ounces of bread in a week, or 21 ounces a day . . . and nothing for drink, fuel, clothing or lodging."

The authorities fumbled for a solution. Back in the late eighteenth century, the Agricultural Revolution had already reduced the farm labourer's staple diet to bread and cheese, washed down with tea or beer. He seldom saw meat, though some were able to grow potatoes in their cottage gardens (there was no room for such fancy things as green vege-

Above. The Agricultural and Industrial Revolutions ended this woman's life as an income earner.

Left. Overcrowded hovels and near-starvation diet were common-place for English agricultural labourers after the Napoleonic Wars, 1815.

The Irish peasant could dig peat for his fire – until the landlord evicted him.

tables). Inspired by this all too obvious plight, a group of Berkshire magistrates held a meeting in 1795 at a northern suburb of Newbury named Speenhamland. They were worried that high prices, married to abysmally low wages, might lead to mass starvation.

Logically, their discussions should have produced a demand for a minimum wage rate; and, at first, it seemed that this was going to be the outcome. However, at some point, they changed their collective mind. Were they being lobbied by local farmers? It would not have been surprising. At all events, somebody persuaded them that, instead, they should urge local authorities to supplement inadequate earnings with contributions from the parish rates. The result was the so-called "Speenhamland Act" (1795), which was established in much of rural England, and was cordially detested by almost everybody. The solvent section of the community disliked it because it put the rates up: the insolvent were equally unenthusiastic. It caused them to feel dependent on charity, which they found degrading: and, in any case, the relief was meagre. Most of them still went to bed feeling hungry.

The Workhouse

The law of action and reaction cannot be relied upon. The Speenhamland effort, for all its inadequacy, was followed by something even worse. Doubtless influenced by an electorate of rapacious ratepayers, the government passed the New Poor Law of 1834. If the Berkshire magistrates had been well meaning but feeble, this was a piece of downright villainy. The nub of it was that the relief of paupers was to become the province of the workhouse – a dreaded and detestable institution, which was run on the lines of a prison (there were some who said that the conditions

The New Poor Law of 1834 created the workhouse

Paupers breaking up stones in a workhouse

in Her Majesty's gaols were, in fact, better). Either a man accepted the puny wages offered by the self-righteous and well-fed farmers, or he committed himself to an establishment which, though it may have inspired some of the best of Dickens, had nothing else to commend it. The theory, of course, was that, if you made charity sufficiently unpleasant, nobody would want it. In Ireland, they did their very capable best to ensure that workhouse conditions were even worse than those of the peasants' hovels.

One particularly vile aspect of the poor law system was the splitting up of families. Writing in 1838, William Howlitt, author of *Rural Life in England*, had this to say: "... till the sound feeling of the nation shall have again disarmed them of this fearful authority, every poor man's family is liable, on the occurrence of some stroke of destitution, to have to their misfortune, bitter enough in itself, added the tenfold aggravation of being torn asunder and immured in the separate wards of a poverty prison." A contemporary ballad entitled "Sons of John Bull" exposed the general situation with telling satire. Thus:

Thy vurkhouses built for the poor, lame and silly,
O who is the covey wot from 'em would part?
The fine suits of grey, and the nice soup and skilly,
The pride and the boast of an Englishman's heart.
O isn't thy vurkhouse a palace of pleasure?
O vare is the country can equal your treasures?
Can boast an assortment of such rags and bones?
Then hail, happy country, bright gem of the ocean,
Such brave sons of freedom the world never saw?

The inmates were either too hungry, too frightened, or too illiterate to make their own feelings known.

In the north of England, things were marginally better, for the industrialists were competing with farmers for employees. The alternative to being starved by a landowner may have been a poor one – but, at least, it existed. In agricultural England, there was no other way.

No wonder there were people who wanted to get away from the whole wretched state of the country in what should have been the beautiful, brilliant and socially enlightened nineteenth century.

In Ireland and the North of Scotland, things were even worse. The potato, that happy harbinger of a full belly, was not nearly so robust as its stolid appearance may have suggested. Nevertheless, the canny lairds and the fly Irish landlords had calculated that a field sewn with this crop would feed more people than an equivalent area of corn. In Scotland, the grain harvest was strictly for export to England. The peasants could stoke up with starch from the thin earth – and like it.

Hunger in Ireland

The Irish peasant was a man of simple tastes, which was just as well. He could scarcely see further than his potato diet: when that failed, his awareness seemed to become numbed. According to a Commission of Enquiry held in 1847: "Provided they have sufficient supplies of potatoes, they are content to vegetate, for they cannot be said to live." At the time, this was ascribed to the Irish temperament. Nobody seems to have suspected that a totally inadequate diet might have been the reason. To say that little was known about nourishment in those days is nonsense. The Irish landlord, usually away in London, would have reckoned it a disaster if he had not sat down to a dinner which, compared with mid-twentieth century quantities, was overwhelming in its scope and volume.

When the potato crop was sufficient, the Irish peasant existed. When it failed, as it did, from time to time, he starved. Even at the best of times, things were almost too bad to be believable. In 1828, for example, Cork

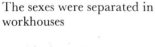

The sexes were separated in workhouses

Irish woman and child begging

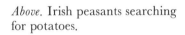
Above. Irish peasants searching for potatoes.

Left. If a landlord ejected his tenants there were only roadside hovels to look forward to.

13

had a population of 117,000. No fewer than 60,000 of them were paupers, and, of this alarming figure, 20,000 did not possess so much as a straw bed. In 1822, during a potato famine, matters became so bad that aid had to be brought in from England – even though, according to a writer in the *Dublin Evening Post*, "The alarming fever of 1822, and the famine which succeeded it, did not arise from want of food in the country, but merely from want of means to buy that food, for we were in possession of a vast quantity . . . The English subscriptions saved a million of people, I have little doubt, by enabling them to purchase it." ("The English subscription" was the money raised in England to assuage the plight of the starving Irish.)

Two years later, a witness before the Select Committee on the State of Ireland said: "The landed proprietors have taken up an opinion lately that the cause of their distress is the over-stocking of their land with people; and, as the leases fall in, they get rid of the surplus population by turning them out entirely from their lands. Those poor people, not getting employment, either erect temporary habitations like sheds on the highway, or they come into towns and crowd themselves into small apartments; perhaps four or five families would live in a garret or small hovel, huddled together there, without clothes or bedding, or food."

Another observer was to say: "Their cabins, which are of the most miserable description, are utterly unprovided with anything that can be called furniture; in many families there are no such things as bedclothes; the children, in extensive districts of Munster and other provinces, have not a single rag to cover their nakedness; and whenever the potato crop becomes even in a slight degree deficient, the scourge of famine and disease is felt in every corner of the country."

Such penury stifled almost every human characteristic but one: the ability to have children. Ireland was overpopulated. The Highlands of Scotland were overpopulated. England, perhaps, was not: but it seemed to be. The expatriate Englishman in Australia had free convict labour. In India, he enjoyed the services of coolies. If he lived in the Southern United States, he employed slaves. Back in the old country, however, there was a home-grown product. Too many people earning too little money provided an endless source of recruitment. The so-called lower orders had never had it worse: the middle and upper classes had seldom had it better.

But was there, perhaps, hope? A nineteenth century writer of hymns, Arthur Hugh Clough, had urged the devout to "Say not, the struggle naught availeth." Very well, then: how did it avail? According to Mr. Clough, "Westward, look, the land is bright." Had he observed the brightness more carefully, he might have noticed that it was slightly tarnished. Still, with no other quarter providing hope, Westward it had to be. Seizing this slender straw of comfort, many set out on what was surely going to be the worst journey of their lives.

"Here and There or Emigration a Remedy"

To the starving, dispossessed Irish, America meant salvation

2　*In Theory*

SOMETIMES IT SEEMED AS IF, for every person who tried to improve his lot by going overseas, there was a theorist either telling him *why* he should go, or else *how* he should go. To a lesser extent, there were also clusters of opinion urging him not to go at all – though, usually, for the wrong reasons. The two foremost thinkers on emigration in the early nineteenth century were as improbable a pair as ever brought their minds to bear on a common problem. Perhaps their closest link was that they were both, by inclination if not by academic background, mathematicians.

One of them was named Thomas Robert Malthus: the other, Edward Gibbon Wakefield. Malthus was born in 1766. He was devoted to his father, who believed in what he described as "the perfectability of mankind." Although he became a clergyman, Thomas seems to have been less concerned with mankind's spiritual potential, than he was about the statistics of the human race. He expressed this in his major work – an essay entitled *The Principle of Population.*

Over-Population

This mathematically minded parson realized what was becoming uncomfortably evident: there were too many people. This, in itself, was bad enough, but it might have been less serious if the output of the farms was keeping pace with the birth explosion. According to Malthus, it was not. As he put it: "Population increases in a geometrical and subsistence only in an arithmetical ratio." In other words, people multiply at a much greater rate than food production. The outcome, unless the former was checked, would be starvation and misery.

Part of Malthus's solution was to discourage marriage and any other relationship which might result in childbirth. He also deemed it wise to encourage people to emigrate. In Ireland, he sadly admitted, there was a strong possibility that nature would do the job more cheaply by starving the surplus people to death. As a clergyman, perhaps, he believed in keeping God's house on earth tidy. For the litter of paupers, there was always, presumably, heaven.

Malthus was said to be "a singularly amiable man"; and, though he feared the institution as a population-producer, he was happily married. If he regarded the colonies as a receptacle for excess inhabitants, he had a formula to back up his ideas. There were also a number of schemes in mind, which were capable of translating his notions into practical terms.

Thomas Malthus said there were too many people, not enough food

You could not throw surplus children (or adults) on to the scrap heap. The best idea, it was thought, was to send them overseas

Assisted Emigration

For people to move their homes overseas cost money. It was an unfortunate fact of life that those most agreeable to going would be those who could least afford the price. To suggest, for example, that a poverty-stricken Irishman should purchase a passage to America, and still keep enough in his pocket for expenses at the other end, would be nonsensical. The poor fellow had not enough for today's dinner – let alone for tomorrow's Transatlantic fare. No: if people were to emigrate (which was a euphemism for "being disposed of"), the state would have to finance them. One plan, which struggled to find favour with Parliament in the early nineteenth century, suggested that funds for this purpose should be borrowed from the poor rate. In Scotland and Ireland, the landlords would be invited to contribute. After four years – by which time he was supposed to have made good – the emigrant would begin to repay the loan. Nobody should be *compelled* to go, though Malthus (and here the mathematician must surely have taken over from the clergyman) insisted that anyone who refused should be denied poor relief. Canada was selected as the most promising target: because it was the nearest colony to the United Kingdom, and the passage was cheaper.

All this pre-supposes that what was good for Britain was bound to be good for other sectors of the English-speaking world. E. Gibbon Wakefield looked at things differently. He refused to see the colonies as a dumping ground to which the unemployable should be sent with the inducement of a financial subsidy and free land. He believed that emigration should be carefully regulated according to the laws of supply and demand for people, and that a man should have to work for his land. In other words, it should not be handed out free of charge, but sold, at a fixed price per acre. The emigrant would therefore have to spend his first few years overseas working for somebody else. If he saved up his money thriftily, he would eventually have enough to purchase his own plot. By then, he would have become accustomed to the farming conditions of the colony in question.

E. Gibbon Wakefield

Wakefield was a remarkable paradox. He was an intellectual who, as a boy, had vigorously opposed attempts to educate him – an individual with an intense liking for the order of statistics, whose early manhood had been a not very creditable example of disorder. He was born on March 20th, 1796. In 1808, he was sent to school at Westminster, where his career lasted for little more than two years. In the autumn of 1808, he dug his toes in and refused to go back. His parents moved him to a high school in Edinburgh, where the results were scarcely better. He removed himself in January 1812 without any clear design for the future. Eventually, in 1814, he obtained an appointment with His Britannic Majesty's envoy to the court of Turin.

Was it because his father was a philanthropist that young Wakefield seemed to think that a profitable marriage was the key to advancing his ambitions as a statesman? His first adventure in this direction took place in 1816, when he ran away with an heiress and ward-in-chancery named Eliza Pattle. Miss Pattle was the orphan of a wealthy Canton merchant.

When the resulting mess had been cleared up, Wakefield returned to Turin as secretary to the under-secretary of the legation. He was diligent in his work, but unchastened so far as his views on women were concerned. Six years later, he decided to raise the money he needed to enter the House of Commons by marrying the daughter of a rich Cheshire manufacturer. Since the young lady was still at school, she had to be abducted: rushed to Gretna Green for an *ex tempore* wedding, and then carted off across the Channel. By this time, her relatives were in full pursuit. They caught up with the not particularly happy couple at Calais. The young bride was sent back to boarding school; the marriage was annulled; and Wakefield was sentenced to three years in prison. During this period, he devoted his intellectual energies to thinking about penal reform and emigration. Appropriately, in view of his status as a temporary convict, he considered the subject as it applied to Australia.

Wakefield passed his days in Newgate Prison, reading everything he could find about colonization, and gradually piecing together his theory. The very crime which had been designed to get him into Parliament, had, by its penalty, ruled out his admission. But this did not prevent him

Edward Gibbon Wakefield believed emigration should be "systematized"

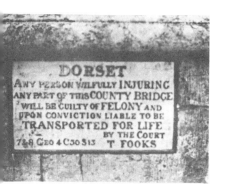

Disposal of unwanted people was well organized in the case of criminals. This notice made the price of vandalism very clear.

from broadcasting his views.

The nub of his argument was that emigration should be state-aided, and that land should not be given away; but, rather, that it should be sold at a fair price. The effect of this would be to improve the input of the colonies. The act of leaving the mother country would no longer be the last hope of the impoverished, the idle and the infirm. A man would have to work to establish himself overseas. Those who had insufficient ambition, and who were likely to become a liability to their land of adoption, would remain at home.

Wakefield expressed this theory, which he described as "systematic colonization," in books, pamphlets and innumerable speeches. It appeared for the first time in the guise of a slim volume entitled *A Letter from Sydney*. It was published in 1829. Since it appeared so soon after the scandal of the Cheshire heiress, and his name was still in disgrace, he used the *nom de plume* of Robert Gouger. This, in a way, was part of the book's strength. He was using a different name and, therefore, he might as well *become* somebody else. Consequently, he told his story as if he were a settler who was struggling to make ends meet in New South Wales. His points were that there seemed to be nothing scientific, and much which was haphazard, about the approach to emigration. Australia in particular was depressed by lack of labourers. The only house and farm servants were convicts, who were not fit for any responsibility. Nor were there enough of them. Here was this rich, succulent, colony, full of promise and with no lack of capital – and yet there were not enough paid hands to deploy its resources.

It was easy to see why. Land was too easy to obtain. The very act of ripping up one's roots and travelling 15,000 miles to an unknown land, suggests a certain spirit of independence. Nobody wished to work for anyone else.

A Letter from Sydney was very readable and persuasive. It was followed, four years later, by *The Art of Colonisation*, which was published under Wakefield's own name, and went into the subject in much more detail. But the earlier work had already made its impact. As a result of it, the National Colonization Society was founded in 1831. The Government abandoned its free-land policy in New South Wales. Instead, 5s. [25p.] an acre were charged, and the money was used to defray the costs of transportation. Wakefield said that the price was not enough; but at least, it was a beginning. In 1834, the South Australia Association was founded to develop the colony: convict labour was banned, and the region was promised self-government when its population reached 50,000. It achieved it at the end of 1836.

Wakefield was not particularly concerned about the poor, and he opposed the pauper system of emigration. Nevertheless, though it may not have been calculated to improve the iot of the colonies, emigration was a tempting solution to the problems at home. Some years later, when the Devon Commission was looking into the question of poverty in Ireland, it reported: "A well-ordered system of emigration may be of very great service, as one of the measures which the situation of the occupiers of land in Ireland at present calls for." Again, the poor rate would be used to speed the unwanted peasants on their way.

R.C.W.

As time went on Australia became less prepared to accept convicts

Penal settlement in Australia

Poverty and Emigration

At the time when Malthus was wringing his hands over the disaster of over-population, and Wakefield was producing his crusading blue-prints for the development of the colonies, successive governments struggled with the linked problems of poverty and emigration. Once the tentative solutions left the lawmakers' hands, they were handled with a criminal brutality. Parliament was, no doubt, more humane (though it was difficult to see the Poor Laws as a blow for humanity): ineffective is, perhaps, a better word.

In 1828, a member named Wilmot Horton introduced a Bill "to enable parishes to mortgage their poor rates for the purpose of providing for their able-bodied paupers, by colonization in the British colonies." The idea went further than, merely, providing passage money. Horton argued that they should be supplied with the capital goods to settle in the new lands: that, rather than become a burden on somebody else's purse, they should be able to create new and potentially affluent lives for themselves. His distinguished colleagues fidgeted through the first reading of the Bill – and threw it out. He tried again in 1830; and, again, the Bill never received a second reading. Two years later, answering a question in the House of Lords, the Minister for the Colonies, Viscount

Emigrants departing

William Cobbett recommended that emigrants head for the U.S.A.

Goderich, said that "he did not think that a necessity would rise for the Government going out of its way to afford pecuniary assistance to those persons disposed to emigrate, as the number of voluntary emigrants to the Canadas had considerably increased within the past year." (The fact that this completely ignored the real problem was not enough to smother a collective sigh of blue-blooded relief.)

The American Dreamland

Emigration was an attempt to escape: from poverty, from disappointment, from frustration. Through the years, the United States of America had come to be regarded as a sort of Never, Never Land in this respect. This was where every pavement was made of gold and where dreams came true. It was, of course, a good deal of rubbish, but the notion persisted for a very long time. One of the people to further it was the controversial writer and politician, William Cobbett. He was not thinking so much of the poor, as of the farmer and tradesmen, and his *The Emigrant's Guide*, which was published in 1829, was addressed to "The Tax-Payers of England."

When he suggested that America was the best place for them, he admitted that: "There is, in the transfer of our duty to a foreign land, something violently hostile to all our notions of fidelity: a man is so identified with his country, that he cannot, do what he will, wholly alienate himself from it." It is hard to imagine that the starving labourer would have agreed with this, but never mind. In Cobbett's opinion, the situation in England was sufficiently unbearable to bolster anyone's will to violate "fidelity." "The state of this country," he wrote, "is now such, that no man, except by mere accident, can avoid ruin, unless he can get at a share of the taxes." He dismissed the deserving poor with the sympathetic and swingeing statement that "hunger, and rags, and filth, are now become their uniform and inevitable lot." For them, then, there was no hope. On the other hand, "for the man who has some little money left; let him take *a calm and impartial look at the state of things* and let him say whether he sees any, even at the smallest, chance of escaping ruin, if he remain here."

One doubts whether Cobbett's look was either calm or impartial. Nevertheless, he made out a very compelling argument for moving home to the United States. He dismissed Canada, because "the whole is wretchedly poor: heaps of rocks covered chiefly with fir trees. These countries are the *offal* of North America; they are the head, the shins, the shanks and hoofs of that part of the world; while the United States are the sir-loins, the well-covered and well-lined ribs, and the suet." He added that: "People who know nothing of the matter frequently observe, that the United States will *take* our American colonies one of these days. This would be to act the wise part of a thief, who should come and steal a stone for the pleasure of carrying it about."

How to Emigrate

So: the U.S.A. it had to be. Although he had spent some time in New York and Long Island, Cobbett's advice on how to get there was based on what *seemed* to be right – rather than on what *was*. Theoretically, there was everything to be said for travelling steerage* and, by so doing, to save some money for expenses at the other end. On the other hand, he does not seem to have realized just how bad conditions in this part of the ship were. For the mass of people who were compelled to travel this way, the voyage was a nightmare. For many, it meant death by disease.

Cobbett never suffered from seasickness: a talent which he attributed to "abstinence from strong drink and to my moderate eating." In this respect, he had original and unscientific ideas. Women were more prone to the ailment than men ("a thousand to one they are all sick together") and servants – possibly paying the penalty of belonging to an inferior class – were worst of all. "They will," he wrote, "be more seasick than your wife and children will be; they will be a plague to you throughout the whole voyage." Leave them behind, he urged.

Strict teetotaller that he was, he also urged emigrants to leave behind their "decanters, or corkscrews; and resolve never to use them again." There was, however, a case for taking along a quantity of brandy. If you travelled cabin class (fare: £35–£40), a gallon was the correct quantity. Steerage passengers (fare: £8 or £4. 50p. for children under fourteen), need only take a bottle. The object, in both cases, was to bribe the ship's cook, who "would bid you toss your money into the sea; but he would suck down your brandy." Once he had been given the chance to suck it down, "you will get many a nice thing prepared by him."

Cobbett argued that American ships were most likely to produce a quick and safe passage: largely on account of their more vigilant captains ("I never knew an American captain *take off his clothes to go to bed during the whole voyage*"). Although, as he no doubt rightly

Steerage passengers. Travelling this way was a nightmare for many emigrants.

* *Steerage* – Part of ship where passengers travelled at cheapest rate, usually above rudder.

observed, "a captain of a ship is *one* man on shore and *another* man on board," the sea-going martinet was not to be feared. In Cobbett's opinion – which was, admittedly, not shared by the majority of emigrant passengers, "You will rarely find him what is called an ill-tempered man." Nevertheless, it was wrong to badger him with silly questions, and "never speak to sailors except in extreme necessity. It interrupts their work and they can't tell you anything useful."

The Emigrant's Guide was merely one voice in a mounting pile of such literature. Though much of it was perfectly sincere, some of the pamphlets put out by emigration agents were travesties of lies – as, indeed, were their advertisements. It was by no means uncommon for the hopeful traveller to be promised a passage in a ship "of the largest class": a punctual departure and "every precaution [taken] to promote the health and comfort of the passengers during the voyage." When he arrived at the port of embarkation, however, he would find that he had bought his passage in a decrepit old vessel. She was about half the size stated in the advertisement: the steerage quarters were inadequate and filthy, and the departure was often delayed for several days.

Later, the emigration confidence trick was applied to land in the new country. Farmers in Britain were sold what were said to be large and fertile tracts in California. When they arrived there, they discovered that they had invested their life's savings in a piece of desert (the promise of oil came later). One ingenious trickster went so far as to invent towns in Texas, which he called by such reassuring names as Manchester, Brighton and Glasgow. None of them existed. As the *London Standard* rightly said: "The emigrants who have already been induced to go out ... declare they were deceived and that the country is unfitted for English settlers of the better class."

Nevertheless, for anyone who chose carefully, there was plenty of sincere advice to be had. There were books and pamphlets and lectures which always seemed to be held at a Mechanics' Institute. One inveterate campaigner was a Mrs. Chisholm who, in 1853, addressed "a numerous audience" at the Mechanics' Institution in Greenwich. Mrs. Chisholm explained regretfully that "most of those who ask me for advice are not young and able-bodied, but men of fifty years of age, who dread the workhouse, which is all they have in prospect if they remain at home."

But the nub of Mrs. Chisholm's address was devoted to the plight of women who were left behind by the emigrants. For example, there were, she said, no fewer than 11,000 husbands on the loose in Australia. In each case, a wife was waiting impatiently in England, expecting every post to produce the money which would enable her to join her man. The money never arrived.

Had the menfolk forgotten to send it? Had they, perhaps, found their status as grass-widowers surprisingly agreeable? If Mrs. Chisholm was to be believed, they were yearning for their loved ones. Unfortunately their good intentions were frustrated by the fact that there was no convenient way of sending the cash. She appealed for some system of money orders in the colonies, which would bring this unfortunate state of affairs to an end.

In the following year, we find this voluble lady again in full blast:

this time giving evidence before the Select Committee on Emigration. The concern of its members was with the appalling conditions in the emigrant ships and, especially, with the outbreaks of disease. Among the points considered were the importance of proper ventilation; of having a medical officer in every vessel of 300 tons and upwards; of producing a proper diet for the passengers; and, for Irish emigrants who sailed from Liverpool, the conditions of crossing the Irish sea. "The seeds of disease," the Committee concluded, "have often been sown among the emigrants by their exposure on the decks of the Channel steamers which convey them to the British ports of embarkation." It recommended that they should be provided with accommodation under cover. Mrs. Chisholm's contribution to the proceedings was to urge that a child of one-year-old should have as much breathing space as an adult. It was clearly a sound idea: but, in the conditions of those days, a manifestly lost cause.

For those who could not read, there was no need to go short of advice. There were always lectures such as Mrs. Chisholm's. For those who could, there was a mountain of literature. Nor, indeed, did it end there. The question was continually being asked: who *should* go? It wasn't, always, a matter of exporting the poor.

Who Should Go?

During the Napoleonic Wars, for example, the local press in the Highlands took the view that people should be dissuaded from emigrating. How much better, the papers said, to enjoy the opportunity of dying for one's country – rather than setting out on an adventure of opportunism. In Ireland, some of the priests opposed it for fear that it would decimate their flocks (in fact, death from starvation was doing it already) and so

Many of the homilies on emigration were delivered at Mechanics' Institutes.

23

Mrs. Chisholm departs for Australia, 1854. She frequently advocated emigration at Mechanics' Institutes.

Some thought Roman Catholic priests in Ireland would oppose emigration because it would reduce their congregations. But many encouraged it.

did the small shop-keepers (though goodness knows why: the lost customers had little enough to spend).

According to one early pioneer of colonization in Canada (Sir John Beverley Robinson, Chief Justice of Upper Canada), the Roman Catholic peasants from Southern Ireland were more promising emigrant material than members of the more affluent society in the north. They had, admittedly, been given to riotous behaviour in the past, but a new life overseas would produce self-discipline. "I know," he wrote, "of no kind of employment so likely to produce this *effect* as labouring for their own *benefit* upon their own farms. Thus, we cannot think it very unsafe to reckon upon a favourable change in the behaviour of those persons, when removed to Canada." On the other hand, the inhabitants of the north, although "better clad and more comfortable . . . more intelligent and less violent, are also, I fear, more republican [*sic*] in their notions." Better, for the sake of the mother country, to send out "poor and priest-ridden" peasants. The Protestant people in Ulster were "independent in mind and circumstances. They think for themselves in matters of government and religion, and too often think wrong."

And so there were theories: hundreds of them. People were told who should go, where to go and how to go. Some of the extremely articulate advisers spoke from experience. They had been overseas and they knew what it was to arrive at a patch of virgin territory with an axe, a spade and a few days' food. The grim voyage was a reality to them: they understood how best to overcome the dangers and the discomforts. But the majority of these sooth-sayers had confined their journeys to brief trips to Europe. Some, indeed, had never been outside the U.K. Their utterances were based on how they believed things to be, and how they thought they *should* be. In the final reckoning, the only way in which to discover the reality of emigration was to emigrate.

"*Emigrating Workman:* 'Goodbye, Mother! Sorry to leave you, but if you can't find me work, what can I do?'"

3 Westwards to America

OF ALL THE COLONIES, Canada was the nearest. It was thinly populated, immense, and it had cost the lives of many British soldiers. The French possessions had been annexed after Wolfe's victory at Quebec in 1759. Later, in the War of Independence, the American colonists had made an ill-fated attempt to add it to the emerging United States. It was obviously ripe for immigration – preferably, in view of the dissatisfied Frenchmen, who lived with resignation and not much else around Quebec and Montreal, by citizens from the United Kingdom. It was an axiom of colonization that, if you filled a place up with the right people at the beginning, you were spared the trouble of sending a gunboat later on.

Unfortunately, Canada lacked the glamour of its neighbour. The United States was seen as an El Dorado: Canada, as Cobbett suggested, was a place where you chopped trees and tried to come to terms with a not necessarily friendly soil. Nor had it the facilities of the United States. Down there, a coal miner, a cotton spinner, or a factory hand could reasonably hope to find work. Up in Canada, it was a case of, literally, starting from grass roots. Pioneers, only, were needed.

One of the government's problems was to persuade people to go there. After all, south of the frontier, the prospect was so much more pleasing. In 1815, an attempt was made to re-direct Scotsmen who were known to be planning to travel to the States. Each was offered free travel, a parcel of land amounting to 100 acres, and free food while he was preparing his farm. Since it was obviously possible that a number would accept the passage, and then travel south to America, there had to be some safeguard that they would settle. Applicants had to satisfy the authorities about their characters, and each had to deposit £26 (£2 extra for those who took their wives). If they remained in Canada for two years, the money was returned to them. Seven hundred and fifty took part in the first emigration. By the end of 1816, the number had reached 1,400, and then the scheme expired from lack of money and enthusiasm. After that, there were no more hand-outs except to a dribble of discharged soldiers.

Ireland had been described as "the wound in Britain's side." If anyone wanted something to worry about, he could always turn his mind to this ill-fed and unhappy community. Indeed, it seems strange that the country had to fight so hard and so long for Home Rule. Considering its record in the nineteenth century, one might have imagined

Opposite The moment may be poignant – but beyond the horizon could be an El Dorado

Leave-taking was a sad
moment. But once abroad
many emigrants encouraged
their families to join them.

that Britain would have only been too grateful to be rid of it.

Canada for the Irish

In 1823, poverty and over-population were, as always, the twin night-mares in Ireland. To relieve both of them, an emigration scheme was devised for "active and industrious men on a system which will best ensure their immediate comfort, their future prosperity." The Hon. Peter Robinson, brother of the Chief Justice of Upper Canada, was appointed to take charge of it. The first party sailed from Cork for Quebec in the ship *Hebe* on July 8th of that year. When they arrived, every male emigrant between the ages of 18 and 46 was given a "location ticket" for 70 acres of land, plus an assortment of essential farming implements and the guarantee of a free supply of food. If they worked the land well for ten years, each had the option to purchase a further 30 acres for the very moderate sum of £10.

At first, opposition had been expected from the Roman Catholic priests, for whom smaller congregations would mean loss of income and influence. In fact, a number of them actually welcomed the idea and encouraged people to take part in it.

The *Hebe* was followed by the transport *Stokesby*. All told, 568 went, of whom 182 were men. There were 143 women, 57 boys aged between 14 and 18, and 186 children under the age of fourteen. The operation cost £12,539 3s. 0½d. [15p.], of which £1,401 4s. 4d. [22p.] was account-ed for by the transatlantic crossing. Later, Peter Robinson returned to Britain to work out a further scheme of this kind. With him, he took a number of letters. One of them was from a man named Michael Cronin to his mother. Let Mr. Cronin tell the story: "We sailed from the cove of Cork on the 8th July and arrived in Quebec on the 1st September. We had a favourable voyage and as pleasant as ever was performed to this country and as good usage as any person could expect.

The newly-arrived emigrant in Canada often started life by felling trees

Then from Quebec to Montreal we came in a steamboat, that is, as I am informed, 180 miles. From Montreal, we came nine miles in wagons to a barracks called La Chingonly, and from thence to Prescott in boats, which is 130 miles. From Prescott we came to a place where we all encamped this month back.

"The whole crew of settlers which came in both ships were sent out from this place in squads in numbers from six to thirty to look at their lands with a pilot to show them their respective lots. It was on Thursday last that I made out my own farm, and as to my own judgement I take it to be as good a farm as any in the country.

"Mr. Robinson, our superintendent, is uncommonly humane and good to us all. He at first served us out bedding and blankets and all kinds of carpenters tools and farming utensils . . . Mr. Robinson promises us a cow to the head of each family next spring and several other things which I have not mentioned now. Since we came on shore, each man is served out in the day with 1lb. bread or flour and 1lb. beef or pork and each woman, boy and girl get the same."

All the letters speak well of Robinson. However, one cannot help feeling that the expedition might have done well to have set off earlier in the year. With the Canadian winter approaching, the settlers obviously felt the cold. As one wrote to a friend who intended to follow him: "I press upon you the necessity of bringing with you plenty of clothes both for bed and body, for that is our greatest want in this country."

Cobbett was anxious that emigrants should leave their decanters and corkscrews behind, and the thought seems to have occurred to one of Robinson's party, who wrote: "I do not wish to encourage my brother John to come to this country if he would not resolve to work better than he did at home. If he would think of coming, and no misfortune has happened since we left home, I think he could bring out some more money with him: he could get land for ten or twelve dollars an acre fit for cropping. If he would keep from the drink, he might do well, but the rum is very cheap (4s. 6d. [22½p.] a gallon) and a great many of our settlers like it too well, which may prove their ruin, for a drunkard will not do well here."

This fondness for the "hard stuff" caused the expedition's one and only blemish. One day, when the Irishmen had been enjoying too much rum, somebody picked a quarrel with a party of older settlers from Scotland. A few shots were fired: when everybody had calmed down, four men were convicted for riotous behaviour. They were each sentenced to two months' imprisonment and fines of ten pounds.

Distance, however, had caused accounts of the affair to become hopelessly exaggerated. There was talk of a complete lack of lawfulness within the Irish camp. They had, it was asserted, created such bad reputations with their neighbours, that the latter were organizing a petition against any similar scheme. In the end, Robinson had the last word. He pointed out that "the disturbance was . . . by no means calculated to injure the character of the emigrants as settlers." Of course, he wrote, "no man can answer that quarrels may not occur – and that there may not be sundry broken heads. No doubt, their children, growing up in the habits of the country, will be more laborious."

All in all, the scheme was considered to be a success, and another was planned for 1825. Within a week of the new project's announcement, over fifty applications had been received from heads of families – each of whom insisted he could be ready to sail at one hour's notice. To the authorities in Ireland, it brought renewed hope. When an Irishman had too much time on his hands, he was liable to express his opinions violently. At that particular time, things were quiet, for most people were busy harvesting the potato crop. As Wilmot Horton said, "Employ-

Cork, from where many Irish left to travel to Canada

ment is a certain cure for the disposition to riot so generally prevalent among the people of the South."

Life in the U.S.A.

America was *established*. The drive to the West had not yet begun: in the east, the trees had already been cleared away – there were industries, established harvests, and fine buildings. The cost of everything was much less than in England. And, for those who were not up to immigration, there were workhouses. They were not a great deal better than those in England, but a man could exist there until the spring, and then be shipped back to the old country. Land was certainly not to be had for nothing; but, almost following the Wakefield doctrine, a man could get a job, work for a few years, and then purchase his plot. Or, of course, he could rent it. As an emigrant from Sussex wrote to his mother and father: "I have a good house and garden, 90 rods of ground, and some fruit trees, for 25 dollars a year."

Another, of a more devout turn of mind, observed: "We are in a land of plenty, and, above all, where we can hear the sound of the Gospel. The gentleman that we work for has preaching in his own parlours, till he can build a chapel; it is begun not a quarter of a mile from where we live – and may poor sinners be brought to Christ; for here is many that is drinking in of sin, like the ox the water." (Both quotes from Cobbett's, *The Emigrant's Guide*.)

In New York, there was a great deal of "drinking in of sin," much of which was designed to rob the emigrant. But more about that later. What seems to be certain is that, in the United States, an industrious emigrant could maintain his family in better style from three days' work a week – than he could by working six days in England.

As everybody agreed, the two most important things were not to hang about in New York, and to get a job as quickly as possible. In the latter case, some emigrants were woefully lacking in initiative. On one occasion, Cobbett was irritated by two passengers who had travelled in the same ship as he. One was a tailor: the other, a collar maker. A month after they had landed, both men called to see him at his lodgings on Long Island.

"Perceiving them to be still as meanly dressed as they were upon going from the ship [Cobbett wrote], I asked them what they had been doing? They said they had been doing nothing: I was surprized, and asked them whether people had left off wearing coats, and horses, harness. They said no; but they could not get as high wages as others got. I found that each could have got a dollar and a half a day, that is to say, [36p.] a day English money, or [£2.02½p.] a week; and that they could have boarded even at a boarding house for eighteen shillings [90p.] a week . . . I advised them to go by all means, and accept the terms offered by the masters; and told them that, at any rate, I had nothing to bestow upon men, who could, if they would, clear their teeth and save 25s. 6d. [£1.27½p.] a week."

Some never succeeded. When Charles Dickens made his tour of North America in 1842, he returned to England in a sailing ship. One hundred people were crowded together in what he called the "little

Lack of industries in Ireland
meant that many Irish
emigrants were unskilled
labourers. So the majority did
labouring work in the
countries to which they
emigrated.

The standard of living was
higher in the U.S.A. than in
Britain. Many immigrants
could therefore afford
to buy the goods displayed in
the shops

Many immigrants started
their own businesses in the
U.S.A. in a very small way

world of poverty" of the steerage accommodation. Nearly all were returning from luckless attempts to conquer the U.S.A. – or, at least, to come to terms with them. Some had spent three months over there: others, only three days. A number were going back, defeated, in the very ship that had taken them out. Nearly all were in the terminal stages of poverty.

Since their fares did not include food, a pitiful few were compelled to live off the charity of the rest. One man – perhaps too proud to accept it – used to make clandestine trips to the galley to steal scraps which had been left on the plates of cabin class passengers. "If any class deserve to be protected by the Government," Dickens wrote, "it is that class who are banished from their native land in search of the bare means of subsistence."

But these were the minority: the submerged tenth of unemployables, perhaps. The majority who travelled to the United States in the first half of the nineteenth century found the country very much to their liking. They particularly liked the outlook which insisted that one should be "courteous, but never servile." After touching the traditional forelock countless times to a self-important English squire, it made a pleasant change.

America's advantage over Canada was that it catered for the emigrant town dweller. One happy little success story is told in a letter written by an emigrant to his father in Kent, and quoted in Cobbett's, *The Emigrant's Guide*. "Philip is apprentice to a tin-worker in the city [New York]; Henry is apprentice to a hatter, about thirty miles from New York; Joseph is gone with James to Albany; Josiah has got a place as hostler about seven miles from the city; I live at 295 Hudson Street, not more than five or six rods from Mr. Selmes; they are great friends to us: *we borrow anything that we want to use of them.*"

Charles Dickens travelled to the U.S.A. and commented on "the little world of poverty" that he saw in the emigrant quarters of the ship.

The writer was learning the carpentering trade. A few days earlier, he had hurt his hand on a piece of timber, but he appeard to be enjoying life. As he wrote: "The labouring people live by the best of provisions; there is no such thing as a poor industrious man in New York: we live more on the best of everything here, because we have it so very cheap."

Another wrote to his children that "people need not fear of suffering; and people are a great deal more friendly than they are, or can be, in England: because they have it not in their power as they have here; for we are all as one, and much more friendly."

New Land in Canada

Meanwhile, in Canada, the battle against nature continued. In 1824, the Canada Company had been founded. One of its objects was to create settlements on a large tract of country owned by the Crown. The Colonial Office, which moves throughout this period with a conspicuous lack of distinction, refused to release any funds for the purpose. By 1827, after a great deal of argument, the company had been allowed to take over 1,100,000 acres on the shore of Lake Huron plus a further 829,430 acres of Crown lands. The territory was to be paid for over a period of sixteen years. Since the land bordering on the lake was entirely un-cultivated, the company was allowed to spend one-third of the purchase

B

Emigrants to Canada.

Emigrants who travelled outside the cities faced a rugged way of life. But the life they had recently left was often even more basic.

money on such public works as bridges, roads, churches, school houses, and so on.

The company's agent in London had been the Scottish novelist, John Galt. Later he was appointed one of the commissioners for the scheme, and we are indebted to him for an eyewitness account of the felling of the first tree at Guelph in 1827. "About sunset," he wrote, "dripping wet, we arrived near the spot we were in quest of, a shanty which an Indian who had committed murder had raised as a refuge to himself . . .

"It was consistent with my plan to invest our ceremony with a little mystery, the better to make it be remembered. So, intimating that the main body of the men were not to come, we walked to the brow of the neighbouring rising ground, and, Mr. Prior having shown the site selected for the town, a large maple tree was chosen, on which, taking an axe from one of the woodmen, I struck the first stroke. To me at least the moment was impressive, and the silence of the woods that echoed to the sound was as the sigh of the solemn genius of the woods departing for ever.

"The doctor followed me; then, if I recall correctly, Mr. Prior and the woodman finished the work. The tree fell with a crash of accumulating thunder, as if ancient Nature were alarmed at the entrance of social man into her innocent solitudes with his sorrows, his follies and his crimes."

Nowadays, Guelph is an industrial town with a population of 51,377. It produces electrical equipment, leather goods, and hardware, and has a university.

As the Canada Company found, the system of granting land in Canada was never simple. According to an Act which had been passed in 1791, one-seventh of all the territory disposed of had to be reserved for the support of Protestant clergy. To make things more complicated, a further seventh was reserved for the Crown. Thus, before anything could be accomplished, two-sevenths of the acreage had to be put aside for the Establishment. It was just the kind of situation that many emigrants had fled England to escape.

But that was not the end of it. Suppose a township was divided up into 200-acre lots. A and B were open to settlement. C had to be put to one side for the clergy. D and E could be settled, F went to the Crown, and G, like ABD and E, was at the disposal of a settler. If the Clergy and the Crown did nothing about their arbitrary bits of land (and neither establishment was noted for its alacrity), the plots owned by honest settlers were punctuated by horrible little patches of wasteland which, as well as being eyesores, hindered the construction of roads.

The situation was ridiculous. The land lay idle for several decades – until 1854, when the clergy reserves were taken over by the municipal authorities. Surely something could have been done about it before this: or was this asking too much? When a government was unable to cope with poverty on its own doorstep, it was, perhaps, unreasonable to expect it to be concerned about some scraps of land thousands of miles away.

4 *The Long Sea Routes*

THE UNITED STATES were the most seductive of targets for the emigrants; Canada was the nearest. The voyage was a distance of about 3,000 miles – compared with approximately 16,000 miles to Australia. No wonder the bulk of the wanderers set out in a westerly direction! Nevertheless, there were other attractions for those who were prepared to endure an even longer sea journey than the trip to Quebec or New York. In 1806, Britain helped herself to the Cape Colony in South Africa. Fourteen years later, Cape Town, which had been a victualling station for ships of the Dutch East India Company, was ceded. The colony was now ready to receive immigrants from the U.K.

South African Pioneers

The initial adventures were not very successful. In 1818, a party of 300 distressed framework knitters from Nottinghamshire landed at Algoa Bay. They became sick, disillusioned, and anxious to return home. Two years later, a landowner named Ingram (he owned 7,500 acres) asked the British Government to export him a supply of labour from England. He was prepared to pay the passage money: the men would serve him for three years, after which they could choose between £10 in cash or twenty acres of land. The government refused so far as the English were concerned. On the other hand, Mr. Ingram was invited to take as many Irishmen as he liked.

Eventually, 420 people responded to his offer. Most of them were illiterate: few had any ideas about loyalty. They broke their bargains; deserted their master's lands; and drifted out of sight into various parts of the colony.

As if the large expanses of land were not challenge enough, there was the problem of the natives. Until the white man arrived uninvited, South Africa had been the province of the Bantus – or, more especially, the Kaffirs. They were a tall, slim, intelligent people. For most of the time, they devoted themselves to farming, hunting, and the raising of cattle. Not unnaturally, they resented the invasion of these pale-skinned interlopers from Europe.

The idea was to contain the Kaffirs to the north of the Great Fish River, which wriggles inland from a point near what is now East London. In 1806, an army officer named John Graham had come out from England with his regiment. Presently, he was given the rank of colonel and put in charge of operations against a Kaffir tribe named the Xhosa.

Top opposite. One in twenty of the emigrants to South Africa was killed by Kaffir raiding parties

Bottom opposite. A new possibility was opened up for emigrants when Cape Town was ceded to the British, 1820

One of his first actions was to establish a site for a military base on the frontier. He found it at a place which was soon to be named Grahamstown. His companion on the expedition was an ensign named Andries Stockenström: a man of Swedish descent who, nevertheless, regarded himself as a Dutchman. Both men were agreed that, although their immediate requirement was, simply, a fort, Grahamstown would quickly become a centre of population.

In their efforts to dislodge the military from their new outpost, the Kaffir intelligence momentarily seems to have deserted the tribesmen. Under the leadership of chief Ndlambe, the warriors mustered in the thick cover of the bush on a day in April, 1819. Had they made their attack by night, they would probably have wiped out Graham's garrison without very much difficulty. Instead, they launched it by day. Wave upon wave of heroic Xhosas, armed only with spears, were mown down by vollies of British musket fire. When the slaughter was over, the survivors retreated, broken, into the bush, leaving a mass of bodies behind them. Grahamstown was secure.

The object of Lord Charles Somerset, the Governor of the Cape, was now to seek an accommodation with the Kaffirs, based on three lines of defence. First, there was to be a demilitarized neutral zone; then the military patrols stationed along the Fish River; and, finally, a population of settlers, who were supposed to be as handy with guns as they were with ploughs. The Kaffirs should keep to their side of the river: the settlers to theirs. So far as possible, the twain should never meet.

Before the scheme could be put into operation, however, the settlers had to be found. Britain had an unemployment problem following the Napoleonic Wars: the economy had not yet learned how to live with the Agricultural and Industrial revolutions, and so where better to shop? Enticing word pictures of a green and pleasant land were painted – whereas, in fact, the acres under offer were an expanse of sandy, not particularly fertile, scrub. However, this was 1819: jobs were hard to obtain and the winter in England was the coldest for years. The Thames froze over at Deptford; the roads were blocked by snow; and the idea of this southern heaven, where the grass was supposed to be green and the sun shone all the time, was appealing. The Government was prepared to spend £50,000 on the scheme, which took it out of the realms of a wild adventure. A total of 90,000 volunteered to go: in the end 6,000 were selected. The head of each family was required to deposit £10 with the Emigration Commissioners before departing. On his arrival in the colony, two-thirds of the amount would be returned to him. Once he arrived at the end of the journey, he would be presented with 100 acres of land – though he was not told where they would be. He had to trust the enthusiastic rumours which were being circulated.

The Voyage to the Cape

A convoy of twenty-one vessels was specially prepared by the Navy Board. Each of them was about 400 tons, and the first to leave was the *Chapman*, which sailed from Deptford on December 9th, 1819. She arrived at Algoa Bay almost exactly four months later – on April 10th, 1820. After that, however, there were delays. Some of the ships were

The worst weather conditions on the voyage to South Africa were encountered in the Bay of Biscay. It was bad enough when steamships were used (as *left*). In the days of sailing ships it was often hell on water.

not ready: others were frozen at their moorings in the icebound Thames. They could not sail until a thaw set in, and it was not until the end of January, that all twenty-one were at sea.

There was heavy weather in the Bay of Biscay. In the tropics, the ships were becalmed, and the emigrants amused themselves by rowing round the stationary vessels in the lifeboats. The conditions on board, although better than on many emigrant ships, were far from ideal. An entry in the log of the *Nautilus* records that: "At four in the morning, we saw the *Chapman*. Later we spoke to her; all well; only lost four children, had nine births." The score, then, was five on the credit side. On board the *Alcona*, however, all was far from well. She foundered with all hands, and one hundred Scottish settlers lost their lives.

Nor was all entirely well with the morale of the passengers. The ships had sailed from London, Portsmouth, Bristol and Cork. Each party had its own leader, and some of the emigrants were recruited as his servants. Unfortunately, when they had been confined in the close quarters of small sailing ships for several weeks, there were rumblings of dissatisfaction. The people in *Chapman* became fed up with a gentle-man named Bailie. There were so many rows that, eventually, they decided to break up into smaller groups and appoint their own leaders.

In the *East Indiamen*, a collection of Irish conceived such a dislike for the head of their party, a former mayor of Cork named Parker, that things nearly reached the point of open rebellion. Thomas Willson in the *Belle Alliance* became tired of "sacrificing myself on the altar of duty for an ungrateful rabble who seek my life." At some point on the voyage, he had himself transhipped to another vessel, and returned to England.

Things were particularly unfortunate in the *Belle Alliance*. Not only were there the angry murmurings: as in the *Northampton*, there was an outbreak of smallpox. However, all was not entirely bad. The Scotsmen, who sailed under the direction of a Mr. Pringle in the *Brilliant*, appear to have been reasonably happy. Even in the *Chapman*, things calmed down when, after a trip of 6,000 miles, the settlers reached Algoa Bay. One of them, J. E. Ford, who seems to have taken over the leadership from the unfortunate Mr. Bailie, wrote a letter of thanks to the ship's master, Captain John Millbank: "We beg to say [he wrote] that the constant and unremitting attention you have shown at all hours and on every occasion have always inspired us with the utmost confidence, and taken from us those apprehensions which the dangers frequently attendant on a sea voyage usually create.

"That you may long continue to have health and prosperity in the profession you do so much credit to, and live to enjoy the fruits of it with your family in great happiness for many years after you have quitted the stormy ocean, is the sincere wish of, Sir, your very obliged servant, J. E. Ford."

Perhaps, looking back on it, the miracle is that there was not more ill feeling. The settlers on each vessel were all huddled close together in the 'tween decks, living as one large family. Many of them were very seasick; and, in addition to the more serious ailments such as smallpox, most of the children contracted measles on the voyage. There must have been many occasions when they thought enviously of the party's leader, who lived in the cabin and enjoyed the delights of the captain's table.

For a more detailed account of such a voyage, we are fortunate enough to have the diary of a ten-year-old girl, Alice Blaine, who made a trip to Cape Town a number of years later. She and her family embarked in the ship *Sutly* at Gravesend on August 7th, 1856, accompanied by their Uncle Robert "who came to see us off." "The ship," she wrote, "was lying in the middle of the Thames, so we were conveyed in little boats to it.

"Much to our amusement we were hauled up the side of the vessel in a sort of cask, open at one side, in which we were seated one or two at a time and drawn up."

The sea in the Bay of Biscay was rough: they were able to make between nine and ten knots, but the highlight in Alice's diary is something which deserved more explanation. "Lord Harding who stands at the head of the vessel," she wrote cryptically, "has lost both his arms during the night." One must assume that the unlucky peer was the figurehead. To lose one arm in these turbulent waters might be reckoned a major misfortune: to lose both of them would surely have caused greater consternation.

Shark fishing was something which helped to pass the time. On August 28th, she noted, "Two sharks were seen about the ship. Mr. Bufsell and Mr. Curtis, two officers of the Carabineers, got some pork and fastened on a hook and threw it out to catch the shark. It kept swimming about the stern and it took the bait and with great trouble was drawn up by the stern until it was dead. It was then brought to the main deck. Miss Fairbank touched its teeth with her finger. She was obliged to put it in brandy to prevent any evil consequences."

There was more rough weather in store. Her brother Arthur and her mama succumbed to seasickness; and, later on, mama seems to have suffered from "very bad headaches." Alice, on the other hand, was a robust young lady and came through unscathed – even after the weather had been so bad that "the water got through the ports in the lower stern cabins so we were obliged to have the carpenter, who put something to keep it from coming in."

The ladies on board appear to have been a nervous assortment of womanhood. Two days before they crossed the Equator, the anniversary of the storming of Sebastopol was celebrated. "In the evening some of the sailors ran upon the poop with a red white and blue flag in their hands, but they frightened some ladies in the *Sutly* so they did not play any games."

Nevertheless, the evening was not entirely spoiled. "They sang and cheered their Captain three times and Captain James three because he ordered them to have double advances of rum."

Alice's voyage took only eight weeks, which was very good going. The settlers who sailed in 1820 were at sea for much longer; and, when they reached it at last, their journey's end was something of an anti-climax. Instead of the verdant landscape they had expected, they found a sandy wilderness, which seemed to extend for many miles inland. According to one report, the first glimpse of Algoa Bay caused gloom "to spread over (at least one female) countenance." Lord Charles Somerset might have described this as the promised land. It was nothing of the kind. Indeed, when they reached the tracts which had been set aside for them, they discovered that a number of Dutch farmers had already turned them down. It was just another emigration confidence trick – designed, in this case, for the defence of Cape Colony against the Kaffirs, rather than for the good of the emigrants.

Ventures to the Interior

In fact, Lord Charles Somerset was in England on leave when the settlers arrived. His place had been taken by an Acting-Governor named Sir Rufane Donkin. Donkin was a soldier who was on his way back to Britain from India, where he had taken part in the Mahratta War of 1816–17. He was said to be "broken in health" and still mourning the death of his young wife. Nevertheless, during his twenty-two months of office, he brought a great deal of energy to his task of helping the settlers – often changing the decisions of Somerset.

The first essential was a new town to act as a trading and administrative centre for them. The original idea had been to develop Grahamstown for this purpose, but Donkin turned the scheme down. It was, he observed, too far out in the bush. To locate an alternative, he sent a Captain Trappe of the 72nd Regiment on a surveying expedition. Trappe selected a point which was much nearer to the coast. It was

named Bathurst after the contemporary Colonial Secretary. Later on, when Donkin had gone, Somerset removed the administrative centre to Grahamstown, which rapidly became a thriving community. Bathurst, simply, dried up. One man who suffered as a result of this, was an enterprising publican named John Jarman.

Deciding that the embryo town could do with some of the comforts of the old country, he built an inn which was originally called the Bathurst Arms. Later the name was changed to Jarman's Inn. It took him seven months to construct and was, by all accounts, a very fine place in which to while away an evening. It should have made Jarman rich; but, when the scene moved to Grahamstown, trade fell off to such an extent that he had to close it down.

But that was for the future: for the moment, the settlers were coming ashore at Algoa Bay, and the builders were doing their best to prepare for them at Bathurst. The former were ferried ashore from the transports in large, flat-bottomed boats. During the final stage, the men and older boys waded through the water: the women and children were carried. Temporary reception camps had been erected round the bay. Later, they all set off in oxcarts for Bathurst, where, presently, the foundation stones of the magistrate's residence and office were laid. The plots for the homesteads had already been surveyed, and the first eight were offered to any who were prepared to build cottages quickly. It was now October: Captain Trappe had been created a provisional magistrate, and all the administration was conducted from a large tent. The work of building went ahead very slowly – too slowly. Many of the settlers had already decided that it was not a very auspicious beginning to their new lives.

Nor, indeed, was it. The first attempts to grow corn were disastrous. A drought was later followed by floods, and the Kaffir population across the river, far from being subdued, seldom missed an opportunity to carry out a raid. The Dutch farmers had tried it already, and moved on to more fertile ground. It was, perhaps, foolish to imagine that the British would fare any better.

Sir Rufane Donkin did his best for the pioneers. Since building took a long time, he provided them with tents on loan. There was plenty of seed and agricultural instruments to be had. His only stipulation was that they might not help themselves to slaves from the Bantus and Hottentots: that, indeed, even the hiring of native labour was to be discouraged.

The next five years were bitterly rough. The tents were replaced by houses of a kind – though most of them were thatched mud-cottages. Vegetables grew all right, but not even Sir Rufane could persuade the land to yield up an adequate crop of grain. Locusts and wild animals did all they could to make life unpleasant: and, where nature left off, the marauding Xhosas filled in with an energetic programme of murder and theft. In 1823, things had reached such a level of despondency that Wilmot Horton, who had been appointed Under-Secretary of State for War and the Colonies, ordered an inquiry.

One of the subjects which came up was that of labour. The English knew the consequences of employing slaves on their estates, but they

Opposite. Algoa Bay – landfall for many early South African settlers

had not been expressly forbidden to use them – and no actual penalties had been established for the crime. According to the official view, they were unlikely to be necessary. "It is," the subsequent report said, "generally accepted that the poverty of the British settlers, and the present enhanced value of slaves [presumably on the black market] have operated against the employment of [them] on their own locations."

There was, on the other hand, little comfort to be had from within the British ranks. "In the parties composed of hired servants," the reported continued, "disputes had early arisen. Tempted by the high wages of labour to be obtained; impatient of the restraints and dissatisfied with the terms of their contracts and, in some instances, with the treatment they received from their masters, the servants endeavoured to secede from their engagements."

"Restraints" probably referred to a regulation dating back to 1797, which required that anyone moving from one district to another should have a passport. Any settler found wandering without the correct papers was liable to arrest. The idea had been to apprehend deserters who had fled to South Africa in the Napoleonic Wars. Nobody seems to have bothered to rescind it.

But, the report went on, "the most pressing and insupportable of their [the settlers'] grievances arise from the constant depredations of the Kaffirs, who have within a few months committed several murders and deprived the settlement of the greater part of its cattle." This was caused by "relinquishing that line of policy, which held out to those tribes a hope of procuring by friendly barter such commodities as their acquired wants have rendered necessary; and which they are now obliged to procure by force or theft."

One settlement, at Fredricksburg, had been burned to the ground.

There was, in fact, a certain amount of trade with the Kaffirs. It was illegal until 1830, when a system of licensing was introduced. Nevertheless, this did not prevent the occasional wagon from foraging to the north of the Fish River. The settlers, relying on the traditional White Man's Magic (which usually came from Birmingham), took with them brass wire, beads and buttons, which they bartered for ivory, hides, skins and cattle. On the whole, they appear to have had the best of the deal. Perhaps the Kaffirs decided it was worthwhile – if only because their goods attracted the occasional villain who smuggled in gunpowder for them. There was one man who had the idea that it would be best to destroy the entire Kaffir nation. In the end, however, prudence overcame his bloodthirsty prejudices when somebody pointed out that, with the Kaffirs gone, there would be nobody left to trade with.

Socially, the settlements struggled forward. In the very early days, an enlightened gentleman named Mr. C. Grubb had started a school for the children. There was no equipment, and so he taught them to write by using their fingers in the sand. When supplies ran short, a pupil was sent down to the river with a box to bring back some more.

With Bathurst virtually abandoned, Grahamstown settled down masterfully to the role of administrative centre for the settlers. By 1823, it already had a saddler, a tailor, a chapel, four churches and a barracks. Seven years later 2,000 wagons were using the town's market, and it was

second only to Cape Town in size. Other villages were established, and the lot of the surviving settlers began to improve.

There were some who did not survive. Between 1820 and 1823, about half the original arrivals had despaired of the unkind land and departed to live in the towns. On a more sorrowful note, about one in twenty of the 5,000 who had landed at Algoa Bay was killed by the warring Kaffirs (or Caffres, as they were called at the time). As in almost every sphere of emigration, the reality never matched the promise.

Destination Australia

If the Cape Colony was 6,000 miles from Britain, Australia was at least another 10,000. When Alice Blaine made her trip to Cape Town in 1856, her diary suggests that she travelled in a well found vessel, probably on a cabin class ticket. For the mass of emigrants, conditions on the voyage were unbearably rough: even on the long journey to Australia – when, one might have imagined, a special effort would have been made to see that the steerage passengers were comfortable. Privately-owned vessels were downright bad: those chartered to the Government were scarcely better.

On January 21st, 1854, readers of the *Daily News* were appalled to

The terrain in South Africa was often hot and unpleasant. But the early emigrants pressed on inland.

learn of the fate of passengers who had left Liverpool in four ships bound for Melbourne. They had, said that newspaper, "been duly packed to the Liverpool system, have arrived after sustaining losses by death which, in a British port, would have compelled a searching investigation."

The "Liverpool system" was a method of cramming travellers into the between decks with a total disregard to comfort, health, and even such elementary human decencies as being able to have a bed to oneself. Something like eight hundred passengers had been put into each of the Australia-bound vessels, with the inevitable result that disease broke out. The *Bourneuf* lost 83 souls; the *Wanota*, 39; 53 people died in the *Marco Polo*; but the worst of all was the *Ticonderoga*, in which 104 died. One of them was the medical officer, and even the survivors had bad attacks of fever. Nor was it any use protesting that this had been an unusually long voyage: quite the contrary. The *Marco Polo* had taken only sixty-eight days, which was the swiftest ever recorded.

According to the *Daily News*, "the cause of this unusual and frightening mortality was . . . the system of packing, which sends 800 in a space not more than enough for 700, and which stows passengers in lower deck berths without any better means of ventilation than a canvas windsail, which cannot be used in storms, when most needed."

When the report was published, the assumption was that this was just another example of private enterprize gone wrong. The ship owners, and those who chartered their vessels, were known to be a mercenary

An early settlement in South Africa

47

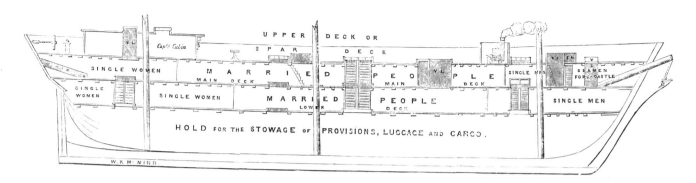

UPPER DECK OR SPAR DECK
Cap's Cabin
SINGLE WOMEN MARRIED PEOPLE SINGLE MEN SEAMEN FORECASTLE
MAIN DECK MAIN DECK
SINGLE WOMEN SINGLE WOMEN MARRIED PEOPLE SINGLE MEN
LOWER DECK
HOLD FOR THE STOWAGE OF PROVISIONS, LUGGAGE AND CARGO.

W. K. M. MINN

A section of the *Bourneuf*, an emigrant ship employed on the Australia run. In spite of careful planning she was often overloaded. On one trip eighty-three passengers died from disease.

crowd of men, who strove to get the utmost revenue out of a passage – without any concern for those who had bought the tickets. However, a few days later, the head of the Shipowners' Association thundered back a reply in the columns of *The Times*. Contrary to popular belief, it seemed, these vessels had been dispatched by the Commissioners of Emigration, which was a branch of the Colonial Office. He pointed out, with an almost breathtaking self-righteousness, that his members advocated 600 passengers should be the maximum. It was no doubt easy to support such an opinion in theory: whether the members would have carried it out in practice is very uncertain.

This was a particularly bad example of illness on the Australian route. Nevertheless, at any time, nobody would have made the journey in steerage for the good of his health.

Archibald Campbell was a warrant officer in the 96th Foot, serving on board the ship *Tortoise* which, in 1841, transported a batch of convicts to Tasmania. In a letter written during the first part of the voyage, he was full of praise for the technical ability of the officers. "With so much accuracy [he wrote] had the ship's reckoning been kept – by dead reckoning and solar observations, that in each instance (viz. at the Cape Verde Islands and the Cape of Good Hope) the time of our seeing land was foretold the preceding day to within half-an-hour of the time when 'Land Ahead' was cheerily sung out from the mast head. Certainly great improvements must have recently been made in the science of navigation, and the instruments must have been manufactured with the necessary accuracy to produce results so amazingly correct."

On the other hand, he found less to admire in "the suavity and urbanity" of the officers. Indeed Mr. Campbell's faith in people seems to have received a knock or two during the voyage. "Such," he told his friend, "is the baseness of mankind in general; so much have I seen – aye, and felt too – of their selfishness and ingratitude; and so seldom is truly genuine and really disinterested friendship to be met with among the sordid inhabitants of this our lower world." Perhaps a convict ship was not the best place in which to seek these qualities. When they reached Tasmania, however, he was delighted with it, and resolved to settle there when he retired from the service.

The convicts, who had helped to pioneer the settlements, continued to arrive until 1867, when the system of transportation was discontinued. The last batch was shipped to Western Australia at the request of the inhabitants, who were short of labour. Only male prisoners were sent there. Earlier, New South Wales had closed its frontiers to the criminal classes in 1836. All told, in just less than one hundred years, the new continent had absorbed 137,161 of them.

Australian Settlements

Life in the Australian settlements during the mid-nineteenth century was rough – and so were the journeys on land. A farmer named Hoddinott, who had emigrated to Melbourne, decided to move 200 miles to a place named Gipsland – taking with him his cattle and sheep. A friend set off with him. "After being on the road eight weeks over the roughest road in the colony," Mr. Hoddinott wrote home to his father, "and swimming several rivers, the other party turned back and left me with my cattle about half way on my journey, having crossed the Irving River, which is 100 yards wide and very muddy. You would think it a fine sight to see 300 head of cattle in the water together, and see 50 stick in the mud . . . getting out and hitching working bullocks on their horns to drag them out. I got every head of my cattle safe in Gipsland after being on the road ten weeks and sleeping on the ground rolled up in a blanket; but it is all over and I am hearty after all, and in a fine grass country and in a fine climate."

Mr. Hoddinott seems to have been his own master. Men working as shepherds on the sheep stations were paid about £25 a year, and received a weekly allowance of 12lbs. flour, 10lbs. of meat, $\frac{1}{4}$lb. of tea and 2lbs. of sugar. They lived in rough wooden huts which, according to another emigrant, were "generally pretty open at the seams. The furniture consists of an old table with a seat. They have a kind of berth fixed up along the inside of huts to sleep in. There are generally two or three in a hut, sometimes more. They have to do their own cooking, which is rather rough . . . For my bed, I had two poles put through sacks, with cross sticks at the ends to raise it a little off the floor. About the neigh-

Convicts attacking a settlement in Australia

An early settlement in
Western Australia

bourhood, there are any amount of snakes, kangeroos, lizards, mosquitos, hornets, parrots and laughing jackasses, and the flying fox.''

The convict servants received rations which were only marginally smaller than those of the free labourers, and they were paid for their work. The story goes that one ex-convict settled down with 3,000 head of cattle after his release. He had purchased them by saving up his wage packets. Prisoners were forbidden alcohol, but the hours of employment were surprisingly moderate. No matter whether they worked for settlers or for the Government, they all packed up at 2.0 p.m. each day.

With so much leisure, it would have been surprising if there had not been frequent outbreaks of robbery. Murder, on the other hand, was rare – and so was sheep stealing. The fact that the latter as well as the former crime was punishable by death may have acted as a deterrent.

Gold Crazy

Sheep and farming were the inducements to go to Australia until the year 1851. In that year, gold was discovered in a creek near Sydney. Subsequent accounts have suggested that the news was kept a secret at first in an attempt to discourage fly-by-night prospectors, and to make

sure that Australia maintained its input of hard working farmers. In fact, according to a dispatch in the Public Record Office, the reason was entirely different. When the first specimens were produced for the Governor of New South Wales, he did not believe in them.

The discovery had been made at Summer Hill Creek – a point 150 miles from Sydney to the west of Bathurst (the former Colonial Secretary's name had a habit of cropping up – whether in South Africa, Australia, or Canada!) It was thought to spread over a large tract of country, and to be of great value. But, the Governor warned his masters in London, "There are circumstances attending the reports which have been made, and the appearance and character of the specimens of gold, which have been forwarded in proof of the veracity of these reports, which lead to a strong suspicion that the accounts of the nature and value of the discovery have been exaggerated . . . and that the gold sent for inspection is really Californian gold."

Meanwhile, a geologist named Stuckbury had been sent by Government House to investigate. Within three hours of his arrival – which may seem to be suspiciously quick – he reported that he was satisfied that grain gold did, indeed, exist in the vicinity. He was not yet, however,

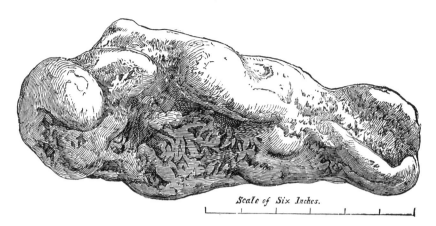

Scale of Six Inches.

prepared to estimate its extent.

A few days later, Mr. Stuckbury was able to report in rather more
detail: there was gold right enough, masses of it. Most of it had originated
in the neighbouring range of hills, and had been washed down by the
rains. Within a very short space of time, the diggings had extended for a
mile up the creek, and anyone with just a tin dish could pick up one or
two ounces a day.

If anyone expected Australia to go wild with delight, he was in for a
surprise. Gold might be the source of wealth, but it also produced
problems. The Governor was afraid that it would "for some time dis-
organize the social arrangements of the whole community and most
seriously affect the interests of every employer of labour in this and the
neighbouring colonies."

The *Sydney Morning Herald* had similar misgivings, though it expressed
them more eloquently. "If we were to say that the colony has been panic-
stricken," a leader writer observed, "that the whole population has gone
mad, we should use a bold figure of speech, but not too much to indicate
the fact. It is as if the Genius of Australia has suddenly rushed from the
skies and proclaimed through a trumpet whose strains reverberate from
mountain to mountain, from valley to valley, from town to town, from
house to house, piercing every ear and thrilling every breast – THE
DESTINIES OF THE LAND ARE CHANGING . . ."

But not, the newspaper warned, necessarily for the better. It had been
a good year until then. The Bank of Australia's enormous debt had at
last been paid off, and "the hopes of the agriculturist were cheered by
the signs which told him that good seasons were returning." And now,

Mining gold.

out of the blue, the gold strike suddenly threatened the *status quo*. One of its first effects was to send prices soaring – some of them by as much as 50 per cent. One prospector had discovered a lump weighing 40 ounces – another, a 20 ounce lump. A Bathurst blacksmith put his hand into a hole and pulled out a chunk weighing 11 ounces. This was all very well; but was it real? Was this manic quest for an overrated yellow metal what life was all about? There were some who doubted it.

Almost at once, workmen threw up their jobs and departed for the diggings. "At present," Mr. Stuckbury was able to report, "everything is quiet. Many people are entirely without food, and stores are not to be got, although I hear that some are on the road which I hope will speedily arrive." Even the surveyor was feeling the pinch. There was no shop in which he could buy a bottle of ink, and so he had to write his report in pencil.

People of all types were attracted by this dream of wealth beyond comparison. A clergyman wrote of the dangers inherent in "many wholly unaccustomed to hard labour, to exposure to the weather, and to the other hardships which they will have to encounter – especially in the winter season of a country so elevated as Bathurst. I cannot," he concluded, "but look forward with dread to the consequences which must ensue."

Every settler had his own solution to the problem. A number advocated the immediate proclamation of martial law. Others suggested that digging for gold should be prohibited for fear that the colony's more conventional industries might suffer. At first the Governor was inclined to take a despairing view of this sudden eruption of providential bounty. As he wrote to London: "I am persuaded that it would be impossible to stop the rush of people to the gold fields without the risk of much bloodshed."

A ''cradler'' for sifting gold

Right: Prospectors lived simply

Below right: Washing the gold

Below: The prospector's lot was often a disappointing one

By May 22nd, however, His Excellency had come to terms with the situation and was able to announce the rules of the gold game. They were that:

1. All gold belonged to the Crown.
2. It was illegal to take gold from the land without . . .
3. A licence which would soon be issued on "payment of a reasonable fee."

The regulations were to come into effect on June 1st. The "reasonable fee" turned out to be £1.50p. a month – and payable in advance. The licences were issued on the spot. To obtain one, however, it was necessary to present a certificate from one's employer, stating that one had been discharged. In other words, the aspiring prospector had to prove that he was "not a person improperly absent from hired service."

It seems likely that the spirit rather than the letter of this proviso was observed. At any rate, there was a large influx from the sheep stations – to such an extent that a hurried immigration of distressed Highlanders from Scotland had to be organized. Having been evicted from their lands by ice-hearted lairds, who had decided that sheep were more remunerative than people, they now had the ironic duty of saving the very species that had led to their ruin.

There was a good deal of irony in circulation at the time. The discovery of gold in New South Wales took place three years after it had been located in California. On the earlier occasion, the Governor of New South Wales had been worried by the number of settlers who had departed for the other side of the Pacific. Now, with its presence on his own doorstep, he did a quick re-think. With a quick twist of logic, he decided that the apparent calamity could be seen "as having relieved it [the colony] of a vast number of desperate and unruly characters, who, if they had remained in it, might, under the present circumstances of excitement, have been found exceedingly troublesome and difficult to deal with."

Within one month of the discovery, there were 1,000 people at the diggings, and this was only the trickle before the flood. In 1852, for the second time in history, more emigrants from the British Isles went to Australia than to Canada. The figures were 32,873 for Canada and 87,881 for Australia. But, gold or no gold, the United States were still the favourite. They attracted 244,261.

Outside view of Australian settler's home

Inside Australian settler's home. It did not compare unfavourably with what he had left in Britain.

The Geelong mail races through Ballarat, Australia

. . . . *And More Gold*

There seemed to be gold wherever you turned. In 1885, it was discovered in the Transvaal region of South Africa. At the end of the century, it turned up in the Klondyke. But this, even though it increased the population to 27,000, was for the specialist. The gold fields which had previously been discovered were accessible. To reach the Klondyke, you had to make an appallingly difficult journey, climb the 4,000-foot Chilcoot pass, and travel by water over countless rapids. It was not for the amateur, who stood a very reasonable chance of being killed if he attempted it. Nevertheless, many tried, and more considered the idea of going. A titled lady in London had plans to set up a store in an icebound habitation of log huts known as Forty Mile; and a clergyman thought of sending his sons out. He wished to be sure, however, that there was a railroad and a post office in the region.

Those who went overseas in search of gold were the opportunists, the men of ambition who had an alert eye for a quick fortune. As emigrants, however, they were the minority. For most people, the long voyage to a new country was a trip in search of hope. They were fleeing from poverty: their only expectations were that things might not be quite so bad at the other end.

Australian "gold town"

5 *Plague and Starvation*

ON A SUMMER'S DAY in 1846, an Irish priest named Father Matthew was travelling from Cork to Dublin. As he passed through the countryside, he noticed with approval that the prospects seemed to be good for an excellent crop of potatoes. As he put it, the "plant bloomed in all the luxuriance of an abundant harvest." A week later, he had finished his business, and was on his way home. Within this short space of time, the picture had changed dramatically. The blight had come to Ireland: there would be no full bellies that year or the next – only anguish and starvation.

The Irish Potato Famine

"I beheld with sorrow," he wrote, "one wild waste of putrefying vegetation. In many places, the wretched people were seated on the fences of their decaying gardens, wringing their hands and bewailing bitterly the destruction that had left them foodless." Ireland was used to disasters of this kind, but this was unquestionably the worst. During the next two years, nearly 700,000 people were to die – either from starvation or from disease brought on by it.

Some emigrated with state assistance. In 1846, 43,439 Irish men, women and children, set off for Canada, and this figure increased to 109,680 in the following year. Many of them never arrived. According to one estimate, no fewer than 17,445 died on passage from fever following malnutrition. The Home Secretary, Sir George Grey, had to tell Parliament that "the Government has received accounts of the most deplorable sufferings endured by the emigrants." This was not due to callousness: it was, simply, that nobody had ever envisaged an exodus on so enormous a scale.

Opposite. Hunger, the ever-present ghost of Ireland, reached unprecedented levels during the potato famine, 1846–7

The potato was the staple of life in Ireland

The system broke down. Something like 700 vessels a year were leaving the English and Irish ports in a westerly direction. They were all crammed beyond capacity with starving emigrants, and it became impossible to find enough surgeons to go round. Many ships had to go without, and the already inadequate regulations had to be relaxed still more. The hygiene of steerage, never of a high standard, became atrocious. According to one eye witness: "No cleanliness was enforced, and the beds were never aired. The master during the whole voyage never entered the steerage, and would listen to no complaints; the dietary contracted for was, with some exceptions, normally supplied, though at irregular periods. . . The case of this ship was not one of peculiar misconduct; on the contrary, I have the strongest reason to know, from information I have received from very many emigrants well known to me, that this ship was better regulated and more comfortable than many that reached Canada."

The Fever Ships

And so the "fever ships," as they came to be called, arrived one by one in the St. Lawrence. About thirty miles down river from Quebec, there was a small lozenge of land, measuring roughly three miles by one mile, named Grosse Isle. Until 1832, it had been uninhabited. In that year, an outbreak of cholera occurred among the immigrants from England and Ireland, and the island was turned into a quarantine station. Previously, the ships had gone direct to Quebec, where a doctor went on board and examined the passengers before allowing them to disembark.

With the coming of these thousands of sick and famished Irishmen, the capacity of this unpretentious establishment was to be stretched beyond reason. The ice on the St. Lawrence had lasted until April in 1847, and it was not until May 4th that the quarantine station was opened for business. Its staff amounted to one steward, one orderly and one nurse.

To squalor the famine now added starvation

Many Irish peasants sought a square meal at that symbol of inhumanity, the workhouse

Irish emigrants escape to the U.S.A. and Canada

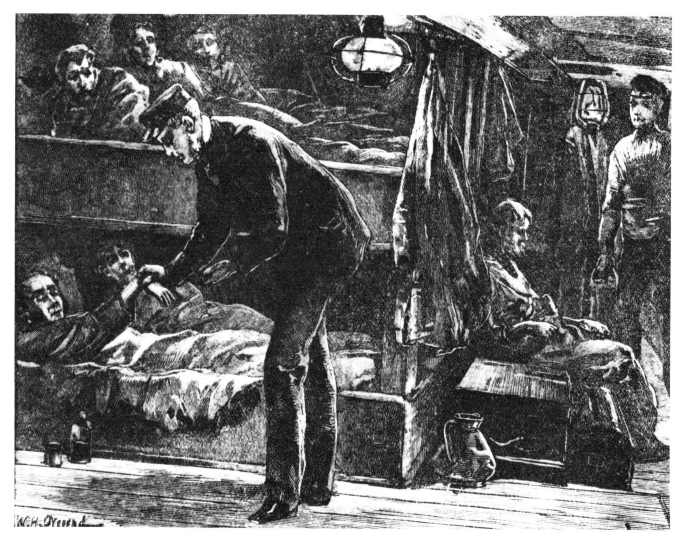

Emigrant ships of the mid-1840s became known as "fever ships". Disease, mostly typhus, was rife on board.

In the hospital, there was room for two hundred patients.

The first fatality occurred on May 15th, when a little girl aged four died of typhus. By May 28th, there were 856 fever and dysentery cases on the island and a further 470 still in the ships. In addition to all this, there were twenty-six more vessels and 13,000 passengers waiting in the river to be inspected. Dr. George M. Douglas, the medical superintendent, was at his wits' end. The Army tried to help by providing eight marquees and 266 bell tents; but, owing to the risk to health, no soldiers were allowed to erect them.

As events moved from crisis to crisis, the scene was described by a visitor to Grosse Isle: "A full-rigged ship is just coming in – not yet boarded. The hospitals have never been so crowded, and the poor creatures in the tents are dying by the dozens! Eleven died on the night of the 8th, and one on the road to the hospital died yesterday morning. Captain Read of the *Marchioness of Breadalbane* died in hospital on the 7th. The captain of the *Virginius* died the day after his arrival. . .

"Since writing the above, we learn that sixty new cases were admitted into hospital and three hundred more, arrived on the 8th and 9th, remain to be admitted."

The writer suggested that it should be renamed the "Isle of Death." "There were 2,500 at that time upon the island and hundreds lying in the various vessels before it. After a long pull through a heavy swell, we landed on the Isle of Pestilence [the idea of the "Isle of Death" must have come later]; and climbing over the rocks, passed through the little town and by the hospitals – behind which were piles upon piles of unsightly coffins. A little further on, at the edge of a beautiful sandy beach, were several tents, into one of which I looked, but I had no desire to see the interiors of the others."

Most of the casualties died of typhus, which had been brought on board the ships by lice. If Grosse Isle was an inadequate reception station, the facilities for dispatching the emigrants from Ireland had been non-existent. If only it had been possible to give them baths and disinfect them, it might have been a very different story.

It was, perhaps, a question of going from one hell to another. The situation in the former was more than adequately summed up in "A Petition from the Irish Poor to the Right Honourable Lords Temporal and Spiritual" at Westminster. There were eighty-six signatures to the document, part of which reads like this:

"In times past the poor of this country had large gardens of potatoes, and as much conacre as supported them for nearly the whole year, and when they had no employment from the farmers they were working for themselves, and when they had no employment they had their own provisions; but now there are thousands and tens of thousands that have not a cabbage plant in the ground; so we hope that ye will be so charitable as to send us to America, and give us land according to our families, and

Grosse Isle in the St. Lawrence River, Canada where there was a quarantine station for emigrants

anything else ye will give us (and we will do with the coarsest kind). We will repay the same, with the interest thereof, as the Government will direct."

Little did they realise what this rush of state-aided emigration was going to lead to. When it was all over, a monument was erected on the site of Grosse Isle's main cemetery. One side of it had these words engraved upon it:

"In this secluded spot lie the mortal remains of the 5,424 persons who flying from Pestilence and Famine in Ireland in the year 1847 found in America but a Grave."

The island was closed as a quarantine station in 1937. By that time, 11,000 had been buried there.

Starvation in the Highlands

The British Isles contained a fat core of industrial prosperity surrounded by countless square miles of poverty. The plight of the Irish was bad enough: that of the Highlanders was scarcely better. The blight which had stricken the Irish potatoes moved on over the Scottish Lowlands, where it inflicted damage estimated at £50,000. Then it travelled north. By early September, it had reached the Orkneys. Since about half of Scotland lived on potatoes for nine months of the year, it was obvious that things were going to become very bad indeed.

When Westminster was asked for help, the reaction was "let them eat oats." This might have meant something, if there had been any attempt to keep the oat crop *in* Scotland. As it was, farmers in Rosshire were making a handsome profit out of selling grain to the English, and they meant to go on doing so. What was a little starvation among neighbours? They even had the temerity to ask for military protection to ensure that their convoys to England were not pillaged by starving peasants. The authorities, seemingly insensitive to the majority's plight, provided it.

By 1849, 3,000 people in Western Ross were on relief, and so were 5,000 on Skye. Many families were living on handouts sent from Canada, Australia and South Africa. Nor was the situation improved by the dispatch of Irish reinforcements to quell the food riots which were occurring. Was this done without thinking, or was it some cruel joke? The sheer callousness of it makes one wonder.

The fact of the matter was that nobody really wanted the Highlanders. As the big landowners had found out, sheep farmers paid two or three times as much rent as a crofter – and they paid punctually. If the latter died of starvation, that was too bad. If he decided to emigrate: fine! When there was a war on, the Highlander showed himself to be a fine warrior, and he was much in demand. In peace, he cluttered up good grazing land, and was better off elsewhere. During the first three years of the nineteenth century, 10,000 of them left for Nova Scotia and Upper Canada – turned out of their homes by harsh landlords and profit-making sheep.

Several nasty little catch-phrases were being coined, such as "The Highlanders are always lazy" – and (from Sir Charles Trevelyan, Assistant-Secretary to the Treasury), "Dependence on charity is not to be made an agreeable mode of life." Even the local newspaper came up with

Departure of the emigrant ship *Hercules* from the Isle of Skye, 1853.

an unpleasant homily on the subject of emigration. "Highlanders [it said], it is well known, can exist on very little when necessity requires them to do so. If each grown person, therefore, lays in one boll of oatmeal, and another of potatoes, there is no fear of his starving and thus, for somewhat less than £4, he will reach the promised land." That he would arrive hungry and emaciated did not seem to bother the paper.

The words were those of the *Inverness Courier*, which had been quick to realize that the Highlands were overpopulated, and equally quick to espouse the cause of emigration. Possibly the fact that the latter attracted advertizing revenue may have helped: at any rate, it once referred to "two respectable agents who, partly as a trading speculation and partly as an act of philanthropy. . ." Trading speculation? Certainly. Act of philanthropy? Twaddle! Admittedly, the advertisement read well enough, with its reference to "A substantial coppered Fast Sailing Ship . . ." and its insistence that "All those who wish to emigrate to these parts [Canada] in Summer will find this an excellent opportunity, as every attention will be paid to the comfort of Passengers, and they may depend on the utmost punctuality as to date of sailing." If other advertizing of this nature was anything to go by, it was all a pack of lies. A more accurate impression of the vessel was probably given by William Huskisson, Governor General of British North America, who witnessed the arrival of the brig *Jane* in 1826. "I really do believe," he said, "that there are not many instances of slave-traders from Africa to America exhibiting so disgusting a picture." The vessels had grown larger since then; but, as the Irish emigration had shown, there had been no improvement in accommodation.

65

c

Some of the Highlanders went to Ireland to obtain passages overseas: others had less far to go. One port at which many embarked was Ullapool, and the highway to this small town in Western Ross became known as "Destitution Road." When a Highlander agreed to sail, he deposited half his passage money. If he was unable to do this, he sold his property to the agent at the latter's evaluation. He then went back home and waited until the passenger list was filled up and the broker was able to charter a vessel. This usually took several months.

The agent took care of everything. He gave advice about how much food to take for the voyage; he was even prepared to sell the necessary supplies. Since he was able to buy a stone of potatoes for 2p. and he frequently charged his customers 10p., this added to his already substantial profits. Like most other emigrants in the early and mid-nineteenth century, the Highlander was steadily fleeced from the moment of

A Highlander weeps as an emigrant ship departs.

Looking back to the Highlands
he has left.

his first encounter with the agent, until the time he reached his destination.

It was all tremendously sad. The Highlanders loved their homes and their country, and the departure of an emigrant ship was always an occasion for sorrow. As John Prebble writes in *The Highland Clearances*, "The Highlanders were like children, uninhibited in their feelings and wildly demonstrative in their grief. Men and women wept without restraint. They flung themselves on the earth they were leaving, clinging to it so fiercely that sailors had to prise them free and carry them bodily to the boats."

Many of them could not speak English. Since the crews of the ships seldom spoke Gaelic, communications were difficult. Less surprising, perhaps – in view of the near-starvation level of life at home – was the fact that many of the children had never seen a plate before, and few knew how to use knives, forks and spoons.

Eviction

The business of stripping humanity from the Highlands continued. Only the old, the sick and the unwanted were left behind. Death could be relied upon to solve this fragment of the overpopulation problem, and to clear the way for sheep. The rest were wrenched from their holdings and turned loose upon the colonies. During one season alone, emigration went through the Hebrides like a scythe and removed 2,000 people. Many of the departures were extremely distasteful, but none worse than the sailing of the vessel *Admiral* in 1851. The villain of the piece was the laird, Colonel Gordon of Cluny, an avaricious landlord whose instructions were simple: the maximum number of people were to be removed from his domain in the shortest possible time. To speed matters up, the colonel had asked the ship to be sent to Loch Boisdale in South Uist. The inhabitants of the island were assembled on the beach, and some of them were put on board by physical force. According to a contemporary report: "One stout Highlander, Angus Johnstone, resisted with such pith that they had to handcuff him before he could be mastered. One morning during the transporting season we were suddenly awakened by the screams of a young female who had been recaptured in an adjoining house, she having escaped after her first capture. We all rushed to the door, and saw the broken-hearted creature, with dishevelled hair and swollen face, dragged away by two constables and a ground-officer."

Elsewhere, they exported convicts. In the Highlands, apparently, to be alive was crime enough.

Reluctantly, England was being made aware of the plight of people all those miles north of the border. In the same year as the *Admiral*'s departure, the Great Exhibition in London was showing the world how technologically advanced Britain was. Shortly after it had been opened, a letter appeared in *The Times* from "the Widow of a Highlander." She suggested that "might not a table and chair be placed in the Crystal Palace near the refreshment rooms, occupied by some lady, with a money box, to ask for the superfluous pence which thousands who daily visit that palace would gladly give. . . Of the many thousands who visit that wonder of nations, there are few who would not cast their mite to arrest

the messenger of death, now busy among the families of Highlanders."

Many Scottish emigrants went to Canada. They maintained such old customs as observing the Sabbath.

Help for the Highlanders

In September, 1851, the Skye Emigration Society had been founded by the Sheriff-substitute of Skye. Presently, the name was changed to the Highlands and Islands Emigration Society. The object was to procure help for those who wished to emigrate, but had not the means of doing so. "To afford information, encouragement and assistance to all to whom emigration would be a relief from want and misery." Applicants for help were told that everything would be done to help them: but that, first, they should convert all their possessions into cash. In deserving cases, the society paid the deposit on the passage and provided a suitable outfit of clothes.

Eventually, it became the Society for Assisting Emigration from the Highlands and Islands of Scotland. Its offices were in St. Martin's Lane, London. The Prince Consort became its Patron: the Governor of the Bank of England, the Duke of Buccleuch, the Earl of Shaftesbury and Baron de Rothschild were among the members of its Committee of Management. A deserving case was described as anyone who would be "a burden to the British community in the mother country . . . a support to it when transferred to the colonies." Some applicants were nearly refused aid because they looked too robust and not sufficiently destitute.

The *Hercules* first docked at
Melbourne, seen here.

However, Standish Haly, the Society's secretary, was reminded that
Britain had pledged herself to send healthy people abroad, and not to
offload her debris of weaklings.

The society's first ship sailed from Skye for Melbourne in 1853. The
captain had thoughtfully taken on board an extra half a ton of oatmeal
so that his passengers could have porridge for breakfast. However, much
to the consternation of Mr. Haly, no devotional literature had been
supplied. This was quickly remedied when the vessel put into the Clyde,
and a clergyman arrived bearing a large supply of psalm books and
thought-improving tracts. When, finally, the vessel set off on her voyage,
the passengers were all singing the 23rd Psalm.

At Melbourne, they had no difficulty finding work. With the gold boom
in full swing, men of their calibre were urgently needed to replace the
sheep station workers, who had set off for the diggings in search of a quick
fortune.

6 *Lies, All Lies!*

IN AUGUST, 1851, Gulian C. Verplanck, president of a voluntary movement known as the Commissioners of Emigration, New York, addressed himself to readers of *The Times* and other newspapers throughout Europe. He urged all immigrants who stepped off the ship at New York to "make their stay in the city as short as possible, in order to save money. It will generally not be necessary for them to go to any hotel or inn, but the passage-tickets to the interior can be bought immediately, and the baggage be at once removed from the ship to the steamboat, tow-boat or railroad. . . This course saves not only much money for board, lodging and catering, but also prevents many occasions for fraud.

Don't be Robbed!

"If passengers go to an inn or boarding house, they should see at once whether a list of prices for board and lodging is posted up for their inspection, as is required by law. Never employ a cart that has no number painted on it, and be careful to note down the number. Always make a bargain for the price to be paid before engaging a cart to carry your baggage. The price allowed by law for a cartload any distance not over half a mile is thirty-three cents, and for each additional half mile, one-third more."

There were, he explained, two main routes from New York to the interior. One was *via* Albany and Buffalo. The fare to Albany varied from twenty-five to fifty cents. After that, the emigrant could proceed by canal, which would cost him one and a half dollars. The journey would take from seven to ten days. Making the trip by train took thirty-six hours, but the fare was eight dollars. Mr. Verplanck stressed that *no higher prices should be paid*. He also explained that, if they travelled by boat, passengers had to take their own provisions with them. Thus, though the railroad journey might seem to be more expensive, it might, in view of the cost of food, turn out to be cheaper. The boat trip also meant "losing time and being longer exposed to fraud."

The other route, which led to the South West, was via Philadelphia and Pittsburg. The fare to Philadelphia was one dollar fifty cents: again, not a dime more should be spent.

But New York was the serpents' nest. "On arrival here," he wrote, "they should not give ear to any representations nor enter into any engagements without obtaining first the advice and counsel of either the Commissioners of Emigration, or the Emigrant Society of the nation to

The Irishman was the eternal optimist – and at the port of embarkation, habitual prey for the unscrupulous men in the emigrant business.

Right and opposite. For many emigrants, arriving at Liverpool was a bewildering, sometimes frightening, experience.

which they belong.

"Never keep money on your person, or in your trunks. Evil persons may rob you or commit worse crimes upon you. Take it to the savings bank . . . never take banknotes if you can avoid it, until you are able to judge of their value for yourselves, as there are many counterfeit and broken banknotes in circulation." Also "what is called a shilling [5p.] in America is not more than sixpence [2½p.] sterling."

There was nothing spiteful about Mr. Verplanck's remarks: he was not getting at anybody in particular, but he was placing on record a situation which, to many an emigrant, had been disastrous. Anyone who ignored his advice, did so at his peril. New York was just as bad as the remarks implied – and so, for that matter, was Liverpool, the chief port of departure from Britain to North America. The North Atlantic was a large and unfriendly ocean, flanked on either side by a brutal disregard for humanity and even the roughest standards of honesty. The sharks spanned the social scale, from wealthy shipowners and agents at the top,

On landing at New York, the runners would be happy to shift luggage, buy a ticket to the interior, or recommend a boarding house – at a price.

to the meanest crimp at the bottom. The most vicious among this army of shysters were the runners. New York and Liverpool were both infested with them, and it was against them that much of Mr. Verplanck's warning was directed. In many ways, the two sides of the ocean seemed to work together. If, by some oversight on the part of the Liverpool runners, the wretched emigrant still had some money when he reached New York, their American colleagues did their best to remove it.

The Liverpool Villains

Liverpool in the mid-nineteenth century was the second largest city in England, and one of the most prosperous. Southampton had yet to come into its own as a transatlantic port: most of the westbound ships sailed from the Mersey. The ccntre of the town was graced with some fine neo-classical architecture, which seemed to stand as proof of its wealth. Behind it, however, there were acres of slums: mean and dirty streets, where rats swarmed.

One building which, appropriately, had once been the headquarters of the slave trade, was now taken over by opportunists intent on making the utmost profit out of the urge, especially by Irishmen, to emigrate. It was a warren of mean little offices, peopled by shipbrokers, merchants, agents, and other sophisticated sharks. Waterloo Road, which is a grey scar running past the perimeter of the docks, was another stronghold. Here, there were more brokers and pubs and eating houses and provision merchants for passengers in transit. But this was far from the full extent of it. There were dark acres littered with crumbling boarding houses, mean little shops, and the hang-outs of criminal characters – the whole squalid set-up conceived with only one thing in mind: robbing men and women who were already poverty-stricken.

One of the key men in all this was the broker. He either worked for a shipping company, receiving a commission on the number of passages he sold, or else he chartered vessels on his own account. He was represented by agents in towns throughout the country, and he advertized extensively. Nearly everything he wrote was a lie, from the way in which he exaggerated the size and accommodation of the vessels, to his list of sailing dates which was usually sheer fantasy. The ships seldom got away on time: sometimes the emigrants were kept hanging about in Liverpool for days on end.

The passage was no doubt cheap enough. At one time, £3.50p. was the going rate for a steerage berth, whilst a cabin passenger might have to pay something in the region of £40. Between the two, however, there was a world of difference. The brokers made their money by cramming the space at their disposal to capacity and beyond. They made it by chartering cheap vessels, which were little more than hulks. They made it by reducing humanity to the status of things, and packing them on board as they would merchandize from the factories.

Ship brokers were big business men: affluent, top-hatted, characters whom you met in the expensive restaurants which nestled in the shadows of the classical facades. They had comfortable houses on the edge of the town and, from a commercial point of view, connections on the other side of the ocean. The shopkeepers had less style, and few of them had more integrity. Their main crime was that of robbing an emigrant rotten, by selling him inferior goods. There was one retailer who made a habit of providing passengers, according to one of them, with "salt beef three years old and sea-biscuits not fit for dogs." Many others were just as bad.

Runners were at the bottom of the social scale. If the brokers and the

In Liverpool all the dockland streets had a common industry – fleecing the emigrant.

The agent: the arch villain

"Clerk to Emigrant: 'Yes, that's all right for the passage money; and now about your trunk?'

"Emigrant: 'And hwhat would oi be dooin' wid a trunk, sorr?'

"Clerk: 'Oh, to put your clothes in.'

"Emigrant: 'Hwhat! And me go nakud?'

boarding housekeepers were the whoremasters, the runners were the pimps. Although emigrant ships sailed from their home ports, many Irishmen preferred to use Liverpool as the point of departure. They believed that passages were cheaper, and they were certainly more frequent. These people arrived in the Mersey half-starved and more often than not after a rough crossing. They were cold, sometimes ill, and frightened by the great adventure that lay ahead. As they began to heft their baggage on to the landing stage, their first encounter was with the friendly neighbourhood runner: a man with the mentality of a thug, who posed as a cross between a porter and an information officer. He would carry their luggage, recommend accommodation in which to pass the days before the ship sailed, even suggest shops where they might buy provisions for the voyage. Provided they took his advice and paid meekly for his services, they had nothing to fear. If they did not, the thug pushed his way through to the front, and they were probably beaten up. Needless to say, the all too pestering escort took a cut from the lodging house keeper, the shops, and, sometimes, from the ship broker himself.

The Boarding House Scandal

Of course, the man grossly overcharged for his services as a baggage attendant. The boarding houses he so vigorously recommended were little more than overcrowded slums. There was one place which had been licensed for nineteen guests. At the height of the emigration boom, it was not uncommon to find ninety-two sleeping there. In another instance, thirty-two people were crammed together on the stone floor of a cellar without any bedding. The sexes were mixed up with abandon – almost as if they did not exist. One man, for example, was crammed into a cubbyhole for several nights with four women.

There were a few establishments which, though they might seem deplorable by today's standards, were, nevertheless, reckoned to be good value. At most boarding houses, the rate was fourpence a night, and this only included sleeping accommodation. The rate at the Union Hotel, on the other hand, was one shilling, but free meals were provided. Another enterprise had been started in a converted warehouse on the insistence of two Roman Catholic priests. Bedding, blankets and a fire for cooking were available – and the itinerant visitors could even take baths.

Naturally, the runners frowned upon these more enlightened places. They threatened the proprietors with assault. It was an art in which they were extremely adept, for many of them were already running protection rackets elsewhere in the city. Common thuggery was not, of course, the least of their talents. When the occasion warranted it, they could rise to much more sophisticated villainy.

Confidence Trick

Suppose, for example, an emigrant was seen to have some sovereigns on him. They probably represented his entire savings, but who cared? The kindly runner, ever preoccupied with the welfare of his clients, would pass on a useful tip. Did the gentleman realize, he would ask, that they would not accept English gold in the United States? The unfortunate fellow already had more than enough to worry about. This was *too* much. What should he do? Did it mean that he would be penniless when he arrived in America?

The runner was quick to come forward with a solution. By a strange coincidence, he just happened to have some American money on him. He could change the sovereigns into effective currency. How would that

Embarkation in emigrant ships at Liverpool was chaotic. But there was really no hurry – they seldom sailed at the times (or even days) scheduled.

77

be? The man was delighted and the deal was done. The runner departed with a pocketful of gold. The emigrant now had a bundle of notes which, as he discovered when he reached the United States, was virtually worthless.

Sometimes, they sold passages on ships which never existed: occasionally, with the connivance of a vessel's mate, they offered cut-price fares. On these occasions, a party of, say, twenty emigrants would be stowed away on board. Invariably, when the captain checked his list of passengers before sailing, they were discovered. When they protested, and pointed out that they had been assured of a trip by the mate, that gentleman would say that he knew nothing about it. The captain believed him: the emigrants were put ashore without any chance of seeing their money again.

One of the tricks was a very crude form of blackmail. The runners would seize a traveller's baggage, and then refuse to give it back unless he paid a further sum of money. A few were unwise enough to attempt to retrieve it by force. Invariably, they were severely assaulted. Sir George Stephen, a mid-nineteenth century Liverpool barrister and philanthropist, witnessed their treatment of one emigrant. He wrote: "Actually, I do not know how to describe it, except tearing to pieces,

A lodging house for emigrants.

only they do not separate their limbs; but they pull them by the collar, take them by the arms, and, generally speaking, the runners who are successful enough to lay hold of the boxes are pretty sure of carrying the passengers with them."

There were, of course, attempts by right-minded people to protect the innocent emigrant against these villains. They were, on the whole, ineffective. Nor, indeed, was it always easy to tell who was on the side of righteousness, and who was not. For instance, the Liverpool Emigrants' and Householders' Protective Society sounds as wholesome and worthy an organization as you could find. In fact, it was the front which concealed a vipers' nest of rogues. Perhaps the reason was that, when emigration was at its peak, the numbers were too big for anyone to cope with.

Corruption in New York

Corruption may have been rife in Liverpool: in New York, things were no better. If anything, the American perpetrators were even greater rogues. The moment an emigrant ship had undergone its medical inspection by the quarantine officials, they swarmed aboard, powerful, foul-mouthed, desperate men against whom only armed force would prevail. Often eight or nine boatloads were rowed out to a vessel in the

For the emigrant who arrived in the United States during the Civil War, there was always work to be found – in the army.

roads. In many cases, the ships' captains were on their payroll, and instances were reported in which these gentlemen received anything up to three hundred dollars for giving a particular gang the exclusive concession to rob their passengers.

The first act was to get hold of the baggage. Any item which seemed to have a commercial value was stolen. For the rest, the charges were exorbitant. A man was apt to charge £5 or more for moving a few boxes – a job which, in London, would have cost about £1.50. There was no reason why the new arrival should not take his own belongings to a boarding house. The trouble was that he probably had no idea of where to go: and, in any case, the brawn of the runner was enough to rule out any argument.

In his advice to aspiring emigrants, William Cobbett wrote: "The boarding houses [in New York] are of all grades, from twenty dollars per week for one person down to four: I have never heard of any less than that. At these houses, the parties are lodged and boarded, without any trouble at all to themselves; and they are kept, I might say, without an exception, by persons of unquestionably good character. The meals are brought to one general table, three times a day; and the variety and plenty are everywhere pretty much the same; the room and style, and manner, constituting all the difference between the highest and lowest."

Opposite. For some, the voyage ended in disillusionment.

The newcomer to New York was a potential victim for every villain in the city.

That may have been all very true in 1829. By mid-century, however, many of these establishments had come down in the world – morally as well as materially. The runners, of course, took a cut from the proprietors, and things did not stop at Cobbett's "lowest." For those emigrants who had really hit bottom, there was a lice-infested workhouse on Long Island in which one of the leading shareholders was a Liverpool racketeer.

But, having seen the victim to a boarding house, the runner was still not done. Few emigrants intended to remain in New York, and the prospect of a journey to the interior suggested untold possibilities for villainy. The source of profit, in this phase of things, was the sale of tickets. Some were forgeries and, therefore, worthless. Others were only valid for *part* of the journey. All of them were wicked examples of overcharging. When, for instance, the fare from New York to Buffalo was two dollars fifty, a runner would think nothing of demanding seven dollars. Before the railway was established, this trip had to be made in a canal boat, in which conditions were as bad as on the emigrant ships themselves. In his *Passage to America*, Terry Coleman quotes the evidence of a witness given before a committee appointed by the New York Assembly in 1847 to investigate frauds on emigrants in New York. According to this man: "They are crowded like beasts into the canal boat, and are frequently compelled to pay their passage over again, or be thrown overboard by the captain." There must, indeed, have been times when the unhappy emigrant wondered whether the hell he seemed to be entering was not worse than the one from which he had fled.

Mr. Verplanck's words of warning were urgently needed. One only wonders whether the people for whom they were intended read *The Times,* and whether, in a showdown, truth would prevail against the violence that all the runners relied upon as the final argument.

7 North Atlantic Nightmare

THEY USED TO SAY THAT, when an emigrant vessel came up the St. Lawrence River, you could tell her by "the smell alone at gunshot range." It was probably true. All the evidence suggests that conditions in slave ships were far better, for people had a vested interest in seeing that the human freight arrived fit and ready for hard work. The owners of the emigrant vessels had no such inducement.

The Emigrant Ships

The first boom in emigrant shipping took place in 1816, when something like 9,000 people were ferried to America in specially chartered vessels. The demand was so great that almost anything which could float was brought into service – from full-rigged ships to schooners. To a large extent, the needs of North American exporters determined the sailings. On the eastbound passage, a vessel might carry a cargo of timber from Canada, a consignment of flax to Ireland, or whatever. Rather than hunt around for profitable freight for the return trip, it was easier to fill the holds up with passengers. If you packed in the wretched people tightly enough, there was plenty of money to be made. Timber ships were especially good for this purpose, for they tended to be larger and there was more room.

For the few who could afford to travel cabin class, the trip was by no means uncomfortable. The accommodation was reasonably good, and the food, which was included in the fare, was often excellent. In 1832, for example, when the New York packet *Lightning* was a week out from Liverpool, the cabin passengers were sitting down to a dinner which offered a choice of two soups; cod garnished with oyster sauce; a choice between beef, mutton, roast veal or turkey; plum pudding or rice pudding; and dessert. For wine there was either champagne or sparkling hock – according to the passenger's fancy. Music was provided for dancing and concerts; and, for anyone who was not subject to seasickness, the time passed very pleasantly. But, of course, you had to pay for it, and this, in any case, was one of the crack ships on the North Atlantic run.

The Irish peasant, the out-of-work labourer, the craftsman whose career had been demolished by the Industrial Revolution: they went in meaner vessels, at prices they could afford, and in conditions which reflected the low fares. They had to take their own rations, which was all very well if the voyage did not last for too long. The trouble was that

The prelude to every departure was a search for stowaways.

adverse winds could often add a week or two to the crossing, and then they ran out of food. Under these circumstances, the captain was often ready enough to sell them such things as salt meat and potatoes – at a price. In his *America Notes*, Dickens said that "all that could be done for these poor people by the great compassion and humanity of the captain and officers was done." He must have been in a singularly enlightened ship. In most cases, the officers were almost as callous as the brokers who chartered the vessels.

In a pamphlet which advised steerage passengers to know their rights, even if they couldn't enforce them, Sidney Smith gave as an example a case in which the captain used to kick anyone who trespassed to the after part of the deck. Nor were the crews and (on shore) the runners the only characters of whom to beware. "Beside sharpers on shore at both ends," Mr. Smith counselled, "beware of sharpers among your fellow passengers."

Sidney Smith's hints for travellers were among many publications and articles written for the enlightenment of emigrants in the nineteenth century. One of them dealt with the equipment which should be taken on a voyage. The tin articles required were, it seemed, "a water-can to hold the supply of water, a wash basin, baking dish, a teapot to fit into the ship's stove for broth, etc., a can for drinking from, a pot to hang on the stove for heating water, tin plates for meals, small tin dishes for tea or coffee, and knives and forks for each individual. All should be marked; and all packages should not only have locks, but be kept locked

Conditions in the steerage accommodation were abominably overcrowded – in spite of the good intentions of innumerable Passenger Acts designed to improve them.

Somehow, the stouter-hearted steerage passengers managed to rise above the conditions on board ship.

and the keys taken out."

This list of kitchenware suggests reasonable cooking facilities. In fact, due to the fear of fire in wooden ships, the stoves were located up top on the foredeck. Each was housed in a large wooden box, which was lined with bricks. They did not produce much heat, and they were not very effective. "From morning to evening [wrote one emigrant] they were surrounded by groups of men, women and children; some making stir-about in all kinds of vessels, and others baking cakes upon *ex tempore* griddles. These cakes were generally about two inches thick, and, when baked, were encased in a burnt crust coated with smoke, being actually raw in the middle. Such was the unvaried fare of the greater number of these poor creatures."

At seven o'clock each evening, the fires were put out by a sailor, who climbed up the foremast shrouds, and emptied a bucket of water over them.

The shipbroker's object was to
cram as many passengers on
board as humanly (or inhumanly)
as possible.

A deck scene in a typical emigrant ship. Passengers were advised not to waste the crew's time by talking to them.

Below Decks

Below decks, things were terrible. There are many accounts of the conditions: one of them, describing the *Thomas Gelston*, which had recently arrived in Canada from Londonderry with 517 passengers on board, appeared in the *Montreal Advertiser*. This is what the paper's reporter had to say about her: "Besides two tiers of berths on the sides, the vessel was filled with a row of berths down the centre, between which and the side berths there was only a passage of about three feet. The passengers were thus advised to eat in their berths. In one of them were a man, his wife, his sister and five children; in another were six full-grown young women, whilst that above them contained five men, and the next one, eight men.

"These statements are given upon the concurrent testimony of several of the passengers. Fortunately a succession of fine weather enabled them to keep the hatches open; in a storm, they would have been smothered."

The *Thomas Gileston* had been at sea for nine weeks.

Much better was the 628-ton *St. Vincent* which, in 1844, only carried 240 passengers. Their quarters were equipped with tables and benches, plate racks and hanging shelves – and, which was a tremendous step forward, W.C.s for the ladies at either end of the deck. Some effort was made to provide proper ventilation. For anyone who fell ill, there was a sickberth with six beds for women and four for men.

But the *St. Vincent* was an honourable exception. More typical was an account given to a Select Committee by the celebrated philanthropist, Stephen de Vere, who had taken the trouble to travel steerage and see things for himself.

"Before the emigrant has been a week at sea," Mr. de Vere said, "he is an altered man. How can it be otherwise? Hundreds of poor people,

Sleeping accommodation was awful: a steerage passenger was fortunate if there was only one other person sharing his or her berth.

men, women and children of all ages, from the drivelling idiot of ninety to the babe just born, huddled together without light, without air, wallowing in filth and breathing a fetid atmosphere, sick in body, dis-spirited in heart, the fever patients lying between the sound, in sleeping places so narrow as almost to deny them the power of indulging, by a change of position, the natural restlessness of disease . . .''

Disease

Disease! It was the ultimate disaster, a ghost which haunted a great many of the emigrant ships. In 1847, the *Brutus* put out from Liverpool with 330 emigrants on board. On the ninth day of the voyage, a man in his early thirties, who had seemed to be perfectly fit, went down with cholera. He was given rough and ready treatment and, strangely enough, recovered. But, by this time, an old woman of sixty had become infected. She died ten hours after her first symptoms. More cases broke out, and more deaths followed. On one day alone, there were twenty-four casual-ties, but the captain showed no intention of putting back to port. He held on until, at last, the crew became infected. This was too much: he went about and returned to the Mersey. By the time the ship dropped anchor in the river, there had been 117 cases: 81 had died and 36 were still on the danger list.

In another vessel, typhus broke out. A young Scotsman saw 53 corpses, including those of his mother and sister, thrown unceremonious-ly into the sea (you didn't even receive a decent burial). "One got used to it," he wrote afterwards. "It was nothing but splash, splash, splash, all day long – first one, then another. There was one Martin on board, I remember, with a wife and nine children . . . Well, first his wife died, and they threw *her* into the sea, and then *he* died, and they threw *him* into the sea, and then the children, one after another, till only two were left alive. The eldest, a girl of about thirteen who had nursed them all, one

Before setting out, emigrants were required to satisfy the port's medical officers. Normally, however, the doctors were unable to undertake more than a rough and ready examination.

after another, and seen them die – well, she died, and then there was only the little fellow left."

Long Voyages

The regular packets from Liverpool to New York sailed on the 1st, 8th, 16th and 24th of each month. Their average time for the voyage was 38 days; the return trip, which took advantage of the prevailing winds, was usually only 25 days. The fare was 35 guineas, which included wines and spirits. The departures of the emigrant ships, on the other hand, depended on the whims of their captains, the weather, and the number of passages that had been booked. They were much slower than the packets, and between forty and fifty days for a passage was by no means uncommon. One vessel, the *Cumberland Lass* with 139 on board from Belfast, took 66 days. Once the passengers had exhausted their own stocks of food, they bought supplies from the captain. He had only potatoes to offer; and, eventually, they, too, ran out. When, at long last, the ship docked, there was said to be no food on board at all.

But the record in this respect probably belongs to a brig named the *Lady Hood* which set sail from Stornaway in 1841 with fourteen families (78 people). The weather conditions were so bad that she took 78 days to make the crossing. Again, the passengers were in a sorry state from lack of nourishment. Malnutrition, indeed, was popularly considered to be one of the reasons why so many emigrants went down with disease. They just did not get enough to eat and the condition was aggravated by seasickness. On some ships there were said to have been women who, literally, starved to death.

Nor, in spite of the advice of the pundits, did anyone have much choice about the vessel in which he sailed. A certain William Cattermole urged that "Parties going together in the steerage, or half-deck, would do right in closely examining the exact accommodations they are to receive – such as water closets; if they are allowed the use of the quarter-deck; at what time the lights are expected to be out. These precautions may prevent bad feelings on the passage." Clearly Mr. Cattermole had never listened to the blandishments of an agent – or, possibly, he was innocent enough to believe the advertisements which appeared. Emigrants seldom had the opportunity to inspect the hell-ship which was to become their home for several weeks. Mr. Cattermole did, however, give one morsel of good counsel: he suggested that the travellers should take enough food with them to last for ten weeks.

The old sailing ships struggled on across the Atlantic: dirty, disreputable, and loved by no one. In 1847, over 100,000 emigrants sailed to either Canada or the U.S.A., and 17,445 of them died of disease in transit. For 3d. [1p.] a traveller could insure his life, though the small print probably excluded death from illness. Baggage, at $3\frac{3}{4}$d. for every £ of value, was more expensive. Few people bothered with either, which was not surprising. They had hardly anything in the way of possessions, and the value of life was decreasing with every year. At the height of the Irish potato famine in 1847, one observer remarked that "It would, in my opinion, have been more humane to have deprived them at once of life." It is a terrible thing to say, but he was probably right.

Opposite top. The travellers in steerage were responsible for bringing their own food on board. When it ran out, they bought fresh supplies from the Captain – often at outrageously high prices.

Opposite bottom. Emigrants at dinner. It was a meal which was not enjoyed by all the travellers. Some were too ill, or too short of food, to partake of it.

90

Normally, only cabin class passengers enjoyed such luxuries as fresh meat and a proper galley (with cook provided).

It had not gone unnoticed that there was far less illness among the shiploads of emigrants from Germany than there was in those from Britain. The reason was not hard to find: the Germans kept their vessels clean. You could even tell the difference, when the passengers came ashore. They were well-scrubbed: their linen was white and spruce, they *looked* healthy. Why could not British ships be brought into line? In other realms, Britannia might rule the waves: in the emigrant trade, she presided over a sewer.

Regulating Conditions on Board

The authorities took long enough about it; but, in 1848, they published a list of twenty-two regulations "for preserving order and cleanliness." Among them were:

1. All passengers had to be up by 7 a.m. unless excused by the ship's doctor.

2. Before breakfast, all the bedding had to be rolled up, and the personal effects of the emigrants neatly laid out in the manner of a kit inspection.

3. There were to be five sweepers for every 100 passengers. All males over the age of 14 would be required to undertake this work, which they would carry out on a rota basis.

4. Two days a week were to be set apart as wash days: the upper deck, only, was to be used for this purpose.

In addition to all this, the emigrants were forbidden to carry spirits or gunpowder with them. All swords were to be lodged with the ship's master for the duration of the voyage, and there were to be no naked lights. Cabin passengers were allowed to smoke: those in steerage had to bite their finger nails. Finally, Sundays were "to be observed as religiously as circumstances permit."

Three or four "trusties" were appointed to enforce the regulations, and also to represent the passengers in any complaints they might wish to make to the captain. In one vessel, these men received a glass of rum each as a fee for their services.

Some years before this list was compiled, a series of Passenger Acts had been doing their best to improve matters, but they never seemed to reach the heart of the matter. Perhaps it was because they were badly drafted and contained too many loopholes. For instance, the Act of 1828 had insisted that there should be a space of 5ft. 6ins. between decks – but it was not necessary to take beams into consideration. Possibly people were shorter than they are now. Or did they imagine that only dwarfs emigrated? Anyone of average height would have had to spend most of the voyage in an unpleasantly hunched up posture.

In 1835, a regulation stipulated that a surgeon was only required in a ship which carried one hundred or more passengers; that food enough for ten weeks must be taken on the trip; that a complete passenger list must be compiled; and that a minimum space should be provided for each passenger. The inspiration came from the Quebec Emigrants' Society, and no doubt the intentions were very good. In practice, however, the points were mostly evaded.

The question of the surgeon was nearly always a mockery. Fully quali-

The first sight of land was
usually a moment of
excitement.

fied medical men were hardly ever carried: more often than not, the
role was filled by an apprentice whose knowledge of medicine was very
small indeed. On one occasion, a sailor was treated for a broken leg.
When he landed and was examined by a qualified doctor, it transpired
that he had nothing more serious than a bruised ankle.

As for the food, ship-owners found it convenient to ignore the Act, and
nobody seems to have been taken to task about it. Passenger lists were
faked (on one, a woman of 60 was entered as a 4-year old boy); and few
attempts were made to enforce the rule about minimum space. It was,
perhaps, made virtually impossible by the fact that emigrant ships were
not *built*: they *happened*. Had it not been for this brisk trade in humanity,
they would either have gone earlier to the scrap yard, or else continued
to go about their business as freighters. To lavish costly modifications
upon them would have reduced their owners' profits on the one hand –
and pushed the fares up beyond the impoverished pockets of their
passengers, on the other.

But, even if it was not possible to legislate about the standard of
accommodation, it should not have been beyond official ingenuity to
control the number of people who were transported in each vessel. It
might not, you may consider, have been too difficult to stipulate a pay-
load in accordance with the ship's size: to count the heads before departing, and to impose swingeing penalties on any master who exceeded his
quota. But – no! Instead of meeting the problem head-on, the law
stalked round the back and imposed what became known as a "Head
Tax" on all emigrants arriving in Canada. The rate was 5s. od. (25p)
for every adult, or for two children under the age of fourteen, or for
three children under the age of seven. Any captain who falsified his
returns was liable to prosecution, and so was anyone who tried to land

emigrants at an unauthorized place. The revenue was to be spent on hospitals and homes for the destitute in Canada.

Its effectiveness can be judged either in terms of its contribution to welfare at the receiving end, or else on its power to deter the over-crowding of between-decks. In neither case did it serve much purpose. Indeed, so far as the latter was concerned, the big epidemics were yet to come.

The passage to Australia (16,000 miles) was one of the longest taken by emigrants.

Improved Legislation

In 1855, the Americans attempted to improve the conditions of emigrants afloat. The new legislation stipulated that only one passenger could be carried for every two tons of ship: that every passenger must have at least sixteen feet of space, and that the decks should be separated by at least six feet. A hospital had to be provided: the berths had to be sufficiently wide, and not more than two people were allowed to occupy each. There were also regulations about such matters as adequate ventilation, the provision of enough food and an efficient cooking range. Captains who did not comply with the rules were liable to fines of up to 1,000 dollars and one year in prison. A fine of ten dollars was also imposed for every death that occurred on a voyage.

In the same year there was a new Passenger Act in Britain, which was even more demanding than the American regulations in terms of space and maximum numbers. Two years later, the fruits of it became clear. Out of 18,758 emigrants who set out for Australia, only 62 died on passage. The number who sailed for Boston was 16,467, of whom only 22 died; and, of the 4,939 who departed for Philadelphia, there were only eight deaths.

By this time, too, the notorious passenger agents had received their

95

Swiss emigrants, who usually sailed from France, were fortunate. Good trains with comfortable accommodation took them to the ports of embarkation. For the Irish, the prelude to the voyage was usually a rough but cold crossing of the Irish sea.

Opposite. Manning the pumps. In one emigrant ship the pumps were clogged by a sack of potatoes which had broken loose in the hold.

first defeat in a court of law. A widow named Mrs. Byrne had booked a passage for New York in the ship *Ashburton.* She was blind in one eye, and when she went on board, the captain refused to take her. He pointed out that a recent ruling by Congress had forbidden the emigration to New York of anyone who was a "lunatic, idiot, deaf, dumb, blind, infirm, maimed, above the age of 60, under the age of 13, or a woman without a husband having a family." If he attempted to get round these regulations he would be severely fined.

Mrs. Byrne obediently went ashore, where she tried to recover her passage money plus a sum in compensation for what she claimed was breach of contract. The emigration agent protested that he had offered

Another peril which beset
many emigrants was
shipwreck. Between 1847 and
1851, forty-four emigrant ships
were lost at sea

Regular and faster sailings
started in 1840 with the first
steamships

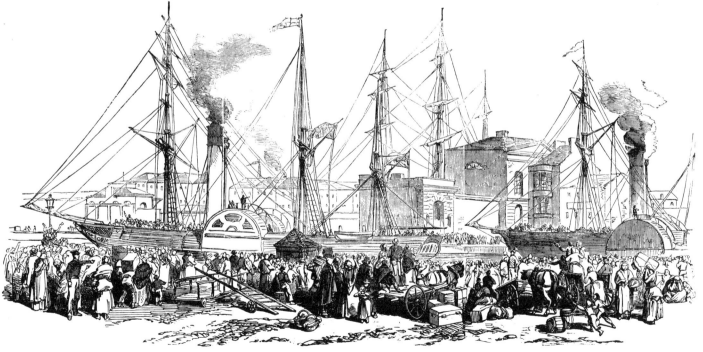

to send her to Philadelphia instead and that he was prepared to re-imburse her for any expenses incurred by the delay. Mrs. Byrne said that this was not good enough, and the magistrate who heard the case agreed with her. He compelled the agent to return her money, pay her £10 by way of compensation, and to provide her and the servant with 5p a day to cover their expenses. It was the first case of its kind. In its way, it was a turning point.

Safety at Sea

Accommodation at sea was not the only problem with which the authorities grappled manfully and, alas, often ineffectively. Considering the urgency of the matter, it is surprizing how long it took to form a reasonable estimate of the number of lifeboats which should be carried. Even when the *Titanic* went down in 1912, many lives were lost – simply because there were not enough lifeboats to accommodate all the people on board. By then, the rules for abandoning ship had been modified to "women and children first." A few years earlier, the priorities had been "women, children, and then first class passengers." This was a relic of the nineteenth century, when life boats had only been provided for cabin passengers.

Every year brought its sorrowful crop of disasters. Between 1847 and 1851, for instance, 44 of the 7,129 ships which sailed from the U.K. to North America were wrecked, and 1,043 people were drowned. In at least one case, the crew abandoned ship and left the passengers to their fate. The fact that the master was afterwards charged with manslaughter was poor compensation for the 196 men, women and children who were drowned. Two hundred and forty-eight people perished in 1847 when the *Exmouth* was driven ashore on the coast of Islay in Scotland; and 176 died within sight of land when the White Diamond Line's *Ocean Monarch* caught fire in the River Mersey. The year was 1848.

Eight years before the loss of the *Ocean Monarch*, however, an event had occurred which, more than anything else, was to improve the lot of the emigrant afloat. The Cunard Steam Ship Line was founded. With the new company came four steamers, each of 1,150 tons, and American competition in the shape of the Collins Line followed shortly afterwards. Steam, which had transformed factories and communications on land, was now making its mark on the ocean. Captains no longer had to wait for a favourable breeze: regular sailings became possible, and the time for the transatlantic crossing was cut to between ten and fourteen days.

Of course, steamers cost more than sailing vessels, and it was some time before this revolutionary form of power affected the emigrant trade. But it happened in the end – and, with it, the North Atlantic nightmare became just a bad dream.

8 *The British Abroad*

IF MALTHUS SAW EMIGRATION as a solution to the problem of over-population, and Wakefield conceived it as the theory of building an effective empire, the various British governments seem to have regarded it as a desperate remedy for use in periods of crisis. When thousands were starving, state-aided passages to the colonies were produced as a panacea. At other times, the emigrants had to pay for their own fares. In any case, the remedy was insufficient – and, it nearly always came too late. It was rather like prescribing aspirins for a man who is suffering from cancer.

The lateness may have been inevitable. If it had been possible to foresee an emergency, the resources could have been mobilized ahead of it. Once it struck, a well-ordered fleet of ships would have been ready to dispatch the sufferers – and, at the end of the voyage, people would have been equipped to receive them. Unfortunately, natural disasters, such as potato blight, seldom gave sufficient warning of their coming.

The Emigration Commissioners

Even in an industrial recession, there was an interval between the cause and the effect. Often, by the time the exodus was at its peak, the crisis was over. Furthermore, although governments realized the need for control of emigration, they preferred to keep the subject at arm's length. In January of 1840, for example, a body known as the Colonial Land and Emigration Commissioners was appointed to take charge of emigration within the Empire. Although they were appointed by the Crown, they were not responsible to the Cabinet. Nor did they have absolute control of the funds for their task. Most of the money was handled by the authorities in the colonies.

The Commissioners had a difficult time of it. There were arguments with the colonies, occasional over-spending, and one of their harder assignments was the task of administering the various Passenger Acts. This responsibility was handed over to them in 1840. Although they tackled it with adequate zest, it was often impossible to persuade passengers to give evidence against offending captains. However, they did succeed in obtaining a number of convictions: enough to serve as examples to the rest, and some improvements came about.

As one colony after another was given self-government, the Commissioners found their responsibilities ebbing away. Nevertheless, there was obviously a need for some organization in Britain which could

Opposite. Agents of the American railroad companies addressed meetings in England to persuade restless citizens to settle on their lands – and, presumably, travel on their trains.

advise prospective emigrants about where to go, how to go, and what to do when they arrived there. When the Colonial Land and Emigration Commissioners were eventually disbanded, their place was taken by the Emigrants' Information Office. It was, to all intents and purposes, a branch of the Colonial Office, and the Secretary of State for the Colonies was (nominally, at any rate) its president.

Labour exchanges throughout the country acted as its mouthpieces. They displayed posters, handed out free literature, and so on. When one considers that, initially, the government only allowed the office £650 a year for all its expenses – including, printing, postage, and administration – one marvels at its efficiency. In 1891, this was increased to £1,000 and later to £1,500. Nevertheless, neither of these sums were princely. The enquiries from the public were adding up to almost a quarter of a million a year. Perhaps the rulers of the realm saw the urge to settle overseas as a reflection of their own inadequacy. If it had not been for the enthusiasm of the office's staff, it, too, might have died from starvation.

Voluntary Aid

Thankfully for intending emigrants, the government was by no means the only source of help. When settlers went to New Zealand between 1837 and 1850, it was largely due to the efforts of E. Gibbon Wakefield and the Anglican and Presbyterian churches. The Salvation Army frequently became involved with schemes; and, by 1886, over sixty different societies were assisting emigrants. They ranged from the Aberdeen Ladies Union to the Self-Help Emigration Club; from Miss J. E. Groom's Emigration Fund to the Winchester Emigration Loan Society. Many of them, such as the Church Emigration Society and the Girl's Friendly Society, had religious backgrounds. Bristol, Brighton, Oldbury, and various parts of London were among the population centres which produced money and advice. Without them, a great many people would have been unable to buy their passages.

The trade union view on emigration was, as happens so often, ambivalent. In Britain, organized labour tended to oppose it, and unions overseas were liable to shut the door (or try to) on skilled workers. There were no such embargoes, however, on the import of unskilled labour. If a man was prepared to work on a farm, he was usually welcomed. Admittedly, there were some unions in the United Kingdom which helped their members to go overseas, but this distribution of largesse was often highly selective. As W. A. Carrothers wrote in his *Emigration From The British Isles* (1929), it was "given only to those who had attracted the unfavourable notice of employers owing to their activity as agitators."

Governmental interest in emigration, such as it was, was mostly concerned with the colonies. The United States, however, was still the favourite target. Even during the American Civil War, when a sizeable number of U.S. citizens migrated to Canada, this trend continued. In 1853, for instance, a total of 329,937 British citizens departed for overseas. Of this figure, 34,522 sailed to Canada, whilst 230,885 went to the States. And, between 1861 and 1870, 72 per cent of all British and Irish emigrants went there.

After the war, the American railroad companies began their huge task

A settlement in New Zealand.

of driving a steel highway to the west. Where the permanent way pointed, the settlers had to follow. What was more, in their acquisition of great swathes of the United States, the railways had land to spare. They not only needed people as potential customers: they were prepared to dabble in real estate. The North Pacific alone sent 800 agents to Britain, and the Santa Fé set up the Anglo-American Agricultural Company with its headquarters in London. Another subsidiary, the American Land Company of London, had 100,000 acres in southwest Minnesota to dispose of. Likewise, the Land Colonization and Banking Company of London was the firm to visit, if you wanted part of 20,000 acres, with town sites and grain elevators – also in Minnesota. One firm opened a travel agency in London. It advertized "cheap and comfortable" passages to America, and was ready to advise anyone who wished to acquire a farm. And, in 1869, an outfit, masquerading as the American Emigrant Aid Society of London, went to the extent of organizing a lottery. The first prize was a free passage to San Francisco.

In spite of this wealth of opportunity and advice, there seems to have been something strangely haphazard about the plans of many emigrants to America. The image was so bright that they might as well have been embarking for Fairy Land: a place which was not only the great provider, but also where every problem had an instant solution. According to Josiah Strong, who published a book entitled *Our Country* in 1885, an intelligent man would go there "with less inquiry as to his prospects in general and as to the particular place in which it may be best for him to settle than he would make if the contemplated removal were, say, from Kent to Yorkshire."

Higher Wages in the U.S.A.

The inducements were much higher wages than in Britain, and the fact that, unlike most of the colonies, the United States provided opportunities for town-dwellers. According to the superintendent of the American census in 1874, "in respect of their industrial occupations, the foreigners among us may be divided as those who are where they are because they

UNION PACIFIC CONSTRUCTION TRAIN 1868

are doing what they are doing; and those who are doing what they are doing because they are where they are. In the former case, occupation has determined location; in the latter, location has determined occupations."

For some, the destination was perfectly clear. If you were a miner, and fed up with conditions at home, the chances were that you would make for Carbondale in Pennsylvania. This, as its name implied, was a centre for coal and anthracite. Indeed, when the first immigrants arrived there in 1827, they were expected to bring English expertise to work on creating "something like a methodical system." Welshmen, in particular, made a success of settling there, and their wives established a local reputation for their neat and comfortable homes.

In 1880, an American mill owner stated that immigrants from Britain can "make at least one-half as much again here as in England, but then they do not live in the same penurious manner. They come here and enjoy rich food, and want meat three times a day, whereas in England they would be satisfied with cheese and porridge." An emigrant made a similar remark in mid-Atlantic, when he said that "in America you get pies and puddings."

One of the results of the Civil War (1861–65) was a cotton famine in Lancashire. Acting, presumably, on the theory that if the raw material could not be exported there must be a thriving industry in the country where it was grown, a number of mill workers decided to cut their losses and look for opportunities in the New World. The Mecca, in this respect, was Fall River, Massachusetts. They used to say that when these emigrants reached "Newfoundland or about there, the first question they ask is, 'Where is Fall River?'" It was the easiest mill town to reach from

For many, in the mid-nineteenth century the way to the West was still by covered wagons.

Opposite top. The building of the Union Pacific opened up the West.

Opposite bottom. From New York the railway was the more expensive way of travelling into the interior.

Below San Francisco.

New York was the most cosmopolitan of cities – nowhere more than Broadway.

New cities were being built in the American West.

New York; and the boat which sailed nightly between the two became renowned for its background music of North Country voices.

There were surprises for both sides: a Kentish farmer, who settled in Texas, was disturbed by the babble of wolves at night. And when, in 1843, a group of English farmers celebrated their first Christmas in Wisconsin, they sang carols in the village at midnight. The older residents, who were unused to this sort of thing, assumed that these strange noises were occasioned by a Red Indian attack. For a few moments, the place was on the verge of panic – until somebody told them about the strange habits of the new arrivals.

Welshmen imported an unfortunate fragment of industrial relations to Scranton in 1871, when 200 of them went on strike. Since Ireland was so lacking in factories, and so few Irish emigrants possessed skills, they were usually relegated to the work of labourers. They looked with envy at Welshmen and Englishmen, who had trades, and who were helping themselves to the better-paid work. At Scranton, thirty Irishmen decided to ignore the stoppage. Going to work one day with a militia escort, a mob of angry Welshmen and their wives attacked them. Shots were fired by the soldiers, and two Welshmen were killed. Later, in a similar fracas, three Irishmen were killed. A meeting of Irish mineworkers afterwards condemned "the premeditated assassination of Irishmen." There would, they resolved, be no more "unity and fraternity with Welshmen in the future." All that remained was liberty: at the time, there may have been rather too much of it in the Pennsylvania mining valleys.

A New Type of Emigrant

The latter days of the nineteenth century saw the arrival of a new type of emigrant in America: the representatives of the British upper classes. These were wayward younger sons, who either had a taste for adventure, or else felt that the family fortune would not stretch far enough in their direction. By going overseas, they hoped to find the prosperity which, according to their view of the situation, was denied them at home. Since the United States was almost a classless society, they had to adjust their outlooks, and become prepared to mix with people who were "not altogether of the kind you have associated with in England." However, they struggled manfully with this difficult assignment, and presently came to terms with it. As one of them said, "They were no longer the same men. [In England], their employers seldom or never spoke to them, and the workmen were rather glad, as they feared the communication would relate to a reduction in wages . . . In Lancashire it never entered their heads to introduce me to their employers. But when I met them in America, they instantly proposed to introduce me to the mayor of the city . . . These men were still workmen, and they did introduce me to the mayor as a 'friend of theirs' in an easy, confident manner, as one gentleman would speak to another."

Perhaps the important thing was, as another scion of a noble breed observed, "you will find that the majority improve very much when they become their own masters and get a home they can call their own."

National Groupings

Emigrants from the United Kingdom tended to form clusters, and they took their traditions with them. The Pennsylvanian coal fields resounded to the melodious thunder of Welsh choirs. For the ladies, there were National Women's Welsh-American Clubs, and the British Empire was not forgotten. In 1909, the Imperial Order of Daughters of the British Empire was founded in New York. By 1916, it had sixty chapters throughout the States.

Northern Irish emigrants took the "Scarf" with them and formed The Loyal Orange Institution, which rapidly proliferated into 364 lodges and 30,000 members – all of which turned out on July 12th to celebrate King William's greatly over-rated victory at the Battle of the Boyne. The Highlanders were quick to form the American Order of Scottish Clans, which became the Universal Order of Scottish Clans when Texas joined in. In Chicago, expatriate Shetland islanders staged the Up-Helly-A festival each year, in which a symbolic long boat was burned.

How Emigrants were Received

By and large, the emigrants were received with kindness when they reached their destinations, though much depended on the state of the labour market. Labourers who were prepared to labour could nearly always expect a welcome. Skilled men who could fulfil a need were no less gratefully received. When, on the other hand, they presented a threat to local talent, and when it seemed that they might force local craftsmen out of work by accepting lower wages, they became unpopular. In the United States, in the belief that North America rightfully belonged to

For Welshmen, the coal mines at Carbondale were an attraction.

Provident societies helped many a departing emigrant to go to the U.S.A. during the Lancashire cotton famine after the American Civil War (1861–5).

Many Lancashire cotton workers left to work at these mills in Lowell, Massachusetts.

the North Americans, there were spasmodic outbursts of opposition to newcomers. One politician who was particularly vocal among the opponents of immigration in America was Samuel Morse (the inventor of the Morse Code), who denounced the flood of foreigners as a certain prescription for disaster. They were, he told anyone who would listen to him, "rushing in to your ruin." In 1891, there were riots in New York against this peaceable invasion, though the rioters themselves seem to have been uncertain about why they were protesting. Nevertheless, they did it vigorously enough: when tempers had cooled, it was found that 141 soldiers were wounded by the mob – 34 civilians were killed or injured.

Earlier, an attack of xenophobia had broken out in San Francisco. In July, 1856, a thirty-five-year old Englishman was lynched after killing an American doctor in self-defence. Had he been an American, he would have received a fair trial – and would probably have been acquitted. In the previous year, 636 emigrants had been turned away and sent back to Liverpool when their ship reached Boston.

And when, in the late nineteenth century, the Australian Labour Party established itself, it promptly urged the government to put up "Keep Out" notices. The theory was that the smaller the population, the greater the shares of Australian wealth. Strikes in 1890 and 1891 helped to harden this view.

Memories of the Mother Country

On the passage out from Britain, homesickness was often added to the

The emigrant's dream. For some, it came true.

Left. The emigrants took their cultures and prejudices with them to America. In New York there were Protestant-Catholic affrays on Orange Day.

Below "The Evils of Unrestricted Immigration".

The first encounter at the end of a voyage was with officialdom, a sad reminder of the land emigrants left behind them.

Ellis Island, New York, – for many, the gateway to opportunity.

misery of seasickness. One Glaswegian observed, on the first day at sea, that "I never shall forget the happy days – particularly Sunday evenings – the western sun shining sweetly in – over the tops of laurel and acacia trees – the blackbirds and thrushes singing sweetly – ah, never, never, shall I be so happy again." Just as the summers of one's youth seem always to have been long periods of constant sunshine (it *must* have rained at some time or another), so were the old dark memories of smoke and slums quickly rubbed out. Certainly, few dwellers in Glasgow at the time would have agreed with this description.

Even later, when the nostalgia had gone, there was an intense loyalty to the so-called mother country. When Queen Victoria married Prince Albert, oxen were roasted in many parts of America to celebrate the event; and when, in 1887, the old queen celebrated her Jubilee, the churches were packed in thanksgiving. The British had a talent for colonization; they even formed little settlements within larger ones.

Within the Empire, the situation was very similar. Not the least evidence of this was the number of Highland Regiments from outside Britain, which fought in both World Wars. There were several from Canada, and a unit recruited in South Africa (the Transvaal Scottish) proudly wore the red hackle, which they had borrowed from the Black Watch. The old cliché, about absence making the heart grow fonder, is often untrue. In the case of emigration, it seems to have a good deal of substance – often unwarranted by the conditions which brought it about. But then children are frequently devoted to parents who have deserted them. The heart is really most forgiving.

9 *The Dawn of Hope*

THE GERMANS HAD A TALENT for dispatching emigrants, and for seeing that they arrived at their destination clean, well-fed and healthy. In 1906, they built an emigrant village beside the Elbe, to which the departing passengers were conducted by cart from Hamburg station. It had a church, an infirmary and a canteen. On arrival, everyone was given a shower and a medical examination, while the baggage was being fumigated. Afterwards, they were accommodated in adequate and inexpensive lodgings, and were able to buy food at prices which would have been laughable to the late and unlamented runners of Liverpool.

Improved Conditions

On the ocean, the Hamburg-Amerika Line pioneered new standards of steerage accommodation, and they were rapidly followed by the White Star Line in England. By the turn of the century, each passenger was issued with one grey blanket and, once a day, the emigrants were sent up on deck while members of the ship's company cleaned out their quarters. But the big breakthrough arrived when the White Star's *Olympic* came into service in 1911, and provided cabins for steerage passengers. Her ill-fated sister, the *Titanic*, was similarly equipped. Everything was changing for the better: emigrants had never had it so good. They were even provided with food from their own galley, and enjoyed the unaccustomed luxury of being waited on at table by stewards.

With the coming of the twentieth century, the British Empire was gradually overtaking the United States as the emigrants' goal. In years gone by, Canada in particular had been regarded as a dumping ground for the half-starved and unwanted. It was a negative attitude. Most people would have been appalled if anyone had suggested that social liability could be disposed of in the way that, years later, Hitler disposed of the Jews. They were, however, prepared to sweep the problem quietly out of the back door, and allow it to settle in somebody else's pile of litter.

Preference for the Empire

But now emigration was being looked at through more positive eyes, and the governments of Canada, South Africa, New Zealand and Australia were helping. In 1909, for instance, the people of New South Wales decided to launch a fund with the idea of presenting a "Dreadnought" battleship to the British Government. Eventually, the idea was abandoned; but, by this time, a good deal of money had been collected. The problem was: how best to spend it? Somebody had the inspired idea of using it to build training farms for boys. Orphaned youngsters were sent out from Britain, educated in agriculture and eventually found jobs.

There were many, similar, schemes. In 1912, a farm school was established fifty-four miles from Perth in Western Australia. The Salvation Army set up another near Rotorua. Throughout Canada and in parts of New Zealand, comparable projects were being developed. Children who had lost their parents could now look forward to a useful and potentially affluent future.

Nor were the unemployed in Britain entirely neglected. In 1928, the Report of the Industrial Transference Board had this to say: "We are justified in expecting that those of our unemployed who are suitable shall be given opportunities and a welcome overseas. It is useless to ignore the certainty that if some of the younger unemployed are to have fuller chances of becoming productive members of the community before the rust of an enforced idleness has eaten into their character, they must be helped to find chances in the wider lands of the dominions."

One of the reasons why the British and Irish people had been good settlers was that they were very good at adapting themselves. In the colonies, they had chopped down trees, cleared away the scrub, built houses and roads in the wilderness. By 1929, at least one writer seems to have wondered whether they were losing this pioneering streak. Wrote W. A. Carrothers, Professor of Economics in the University of Saskatchewan: "The pioneers of today face a different situation from that of

By the late nineteenth century, the lot of the emigrant passenger had improved considerably – though ships were still crowded.

A tender takes emigrants from
Liverpool quayside to join an
emigrant ship, 1913.

their forerunners a hundred years ago. The home is a much less self-sufficient institution economically. We are much more dependent today on the services of people outside the home. The days of the spinning-wheel and the loom are gone. The art of doing what were once simple things in the home is being lost. Consequently people today are not so well equipped to face life in isolation. This means that considerably greater preparation before settlement is necessary."

Still – they got by.

Ideas but no Action

Before the First World War, a number of schemes were put up to the Government – and turned down. In 1906, the author Sir Rider Haggard had been impressed with a couple of settlements founded by the Salvation Army in the United States. Could not something on these lines be carried out within the Empire? The Poor Law authorities were to be asked to finance the project: after all, it would remove a burden, or part of it, on the rates. The assistance would take the form of loans, which the settlers would repay in instalments of £6 a year. About 1,500 families would be involved. No settlement would be of less than one hundred families. As in America, the Salvation Army would train the emigrants for their new work, undertake the transportation, prepare the land for them and build the houses.

The Government replied that it would be difficult to recover the money; that the undertaking was too large and that, in any case, "the arrangement by a religious body [was] undesirable."

As always, the official attitude to emigration was cautious; even chicken-hearted. Nor did anybody seem to be in a hurry. In 1911, it was decided that a Royal Commission should be appointed to study the self-governing dominions as a market for potential emigrants. The members were selected in the following year, and they set off on what must have been one of the slowest global tours on record. One by one, they visited the five dominions. When, at last, they issued their report in 1918, it was nothing if not thorough. But, by then, the war had exploded, and rumbled, and died with a final bang. Among the recom-

Even though conditions were
better, in 1913 the look on the
emigrant's face was still sad.

Not much to look at, but home in a new land – Australia, 1899

mendations was that a Central Emigration Authority should be set up to control emigration from Britain. It would, of course, work in close collaboration with the London agents of the overseas governments.

All manner of objections were raised. Should the authority come under the Colonial Office, or should it belong to the Board of Trade? Would it offend the presumably very sensitive dominions? Even the shipping companies found something at which to carp. An Emigration Bill based on it was presented to Parliament – and thrown out. There was a rash of resignations, and another committee was appointed. It was a game which could go on for ever – provided nobody hoped to achieve anything.

The First-World War

Not unnaturally, emigration came to a standstill in 1914. Several Australian states refused admission to men of military age, and the British government took equal pains to ensure that the exit doors were closed to cannon fodder. For the dominions, this was a serious state of affairs. No new blood was coming in: on the contrary, there was a sudden and large exodus of able-bodied young men, hurrying to support the motherland in her hour of need. With all the young husbands being plucked from the nests, precious few babies were being born.

The aftermath of any war produces a period of disillusionment. The rewards of victory, which the statesmen promise in their recruiting campaigns, turn out to be empty phrases. "The land fit for heroes," which was the slogan of the First World War, became nothing of the kind. Industry, after reaching titanic heights, ran down. The labour market was packed with returning soldiers. Add to this a restlessness produced by service life, and you are liable to find yourself with a flourishing emigration business on your hands. The key to it, as always, is hope: that, when the mother country has failed, somewhere else may do better.

In an attempt to improve the lot of the ex-service man, and to re-stock the Empire, a so-called Free Passage Scheme was introduced when the war ended. Anyone who could show that he was assured of a job in one of the dominions, or who was prepared to take advantage of a scheme for acquiring land, could receive a free third class passage. Ex-service women, and the widows of those who had been killed in action, were also eligible. The offer lasted until 1922, during which time 39,419 (making a total of 86,027 with their families) took advantage of it. As the government took care to point out, this did not herald any change in its views against state-aided emigration. It was an *ex tempore* measure, designed for a special class of person under exceptional circumstances.

America Shuts the Door

One of the more happy coincidences of history was the meeting in London, in 1921, of the Prime Ministers of the various dominions. Having wearied of world politics, and being consumed by an intense nationalistic fervour from within, the ever-open door of the United States was gently pulled to. The "Quota Acts" of 1921 and 1924 ruled that Asiatic immigrants should be excluded entirely; people of Latin, Slav or Celtic extraction might be admitted – though only in moderation. Anglo-Saxon immigration was also to be restricted – but Canadians, Germans and Britons received larger allocations than the other groups. The message was clear. The Statue of Liberty no longer had a notice with the word "Welcome" on it. "Keep Out" was the order of the day. For all but a few who decided to leave the U.K., it was the Empire or nothing.

Empire Settlement Act, 1922

Presumably, the word "emigrant" was too suggestive of destitute Irishmen: at all events, one of the Prime Ministers' recommendations was that the word should be scrapped, and "settlers" used in its place. More important, perhaps, was that, as a result of their deliberations, the Empire Settlement Act received Royal Assent in 1922. As explained at a conference in the following year: "The primary object of the new policy is to promote the development of Empire production and con-

Posters pointed the way to Canada – and offered opportunities at very low rates.

The horrors of the First World War (portrayed here by Paul Nash) caused people to seek happier lives abroad.

There is a happy land, far, far away . . . or so the Canadian Pacific Railway suggested.

sequently of Empire trade. A growing population overseas is a necessary condition and concomitant of the development of Empire production. It is not the only factor, since movement of population cannot by itself be effective unless the settlers are able to make good and to find markets for the produce of their labour . . . The new policy, therefore, aims at remedying the shortage of white population overseas and at diminishing in some degree the present excessive inequality of distribution of the white population of the Empire." In a jumble of official syntax, the paper went on to stress how important it was that the bulk of the Empire's population "shall be retained under the British flag." It also made very clear that the Act was not to be "looked upon as a remedy for the immediate abnormal unemployment in this country."

Beneath all this verbiage, the Act had a heart of gold. At last, after goodness how many years, state-aided emigration (correction: perhaps we had now better call it "settlement") was to be introduced on a larger and more enduring scale. The expenditure was to be split on a 50/50

The Empire Settlement Plan
aimed to keep the Empire
white – even in Canada, where
the problem did not really
arise.

Prosperity in Canada was a
horse, a cow and a few acres.

Above and opposite. In the 1930s
unemployment in Britain
drove more people abroad.

basis with the dominions' governments: the help was available to anyone
"who intended to settle in any part of His Majesty's Overseas Dominions." It would assist with passages, provide training for re-settlement,
and pay out initial allowances to tide people over until they became
established – all this provided the dominions paid up their shares of the
expenditure and that the scheme did not cost the British Exchequer more
than £3 million a year. The Act would remain in force for fifteen years.

It was rather like re-stocking rivers with the right kind of trout, but
at least it was something. Among those who raised their voices in praise
of it was Lord Long, a former Secretary of State for the Colonies.
"I particularly rejoice that the Government have produced a scheme
of this kind," His Lordship said, "because it is the first time that any
Government in this country has recognized the plain fact which stares
us all in the face, though we may not hitherto have cared to realize it,
that if you are going to deal with the growing population of this country,
with its limitation of area, and consequently to a large extent limitation
of employment, you can only do so by a wise, generous and well thought-
out scheme of migration."

It may not have been precisely what the compilers of the Act had in
mind, but nobody could deny the truth of it. The first results were seen
later that year, when 14,099 people were helped on their way to Australia
and New Zealand at a cost of £35,464. Four and a half years later,
189,000 had been assisted at the rate of about 42,000 a year. Nevertheless, it was pointed out that this was merely toying with the real problem.
It might be helping individuals to move to new homes overseas; but, as

a method of re-distributing the white population of the Empire, it was not going nearly far enough. Everything, of course, has its price. According to one school of thought, the sum available was nothing like sufficient – £200 million would have been a more realistic estimate.

The unemployment, which Lord Long had envisaged, was about to arrive with a vengeance. By 1929, there were 947,000 men out of work in Great Britain and Northern Ireland. Two years later, the figure had become 2,127,000 and it was still rising. And yet, in 1928, the Prime Minister, Stanley Baldwin, told the House of Commons that, although the Overseas Dominions had great possibilities "for a very large number of men who are willing to turn their hand to the first job that comes along and to work hard; but they feel that the intervention of governments, with all the caution that is involved owing to political considerations, is gradually turning the idea of a courageous adventure – with a big chance of success, even if there may be some risk of failure – into a slow and restricted policy of migration confined to guaranteed employment. It is not in this way that the Dominions were built up, nor is this the way that they will attract large numbers of British people."

It was not indeed: it was through poverty and starvation and fever ships and absentee landlords and men who preferred sheep to human beings. Indeed, if anybody is looking for a miracle, he might do worse than consider that, out of these squalid circumstances, through the pipe-line of suffering that was emigration, such fine and powerful nations as Canada and Australia, New Zealand and, to a lesser extent, South Africa emerged. There was precious little "intervention of governments." Perhaps, if they had been able to leave "political considerations" alone for a while, it might have been better if they had intervened.

The Last Resort

To go back to the beginning: Malthus wished to correct alarming over-population trends; Wakefield was determined to build what he regarded as the right kind of Empire by his theory of "systematic colonizers." The one regarded colonies as dumping grounds: the other saw them as vast building sites to be peopled by the fit and the ambitious. What a pity that neither of these important thinkers seems to have spared a thought for the poor devil who was perplexed, hungry, a prey for every vulture in the business, who had been compelled to leave his home for the dubious delights of roughing it in some unknown land. Emigration is about people: a fact which, far too often, seems to have been forgotten.

As a remedy: too little, too late. In 1928, the Government must have seen the way things were heading. The great depression did not arrive out of the blue. In the following year, the slump hit Wall Street and the germs of the greatest industrial disease of all time were being blown across the Atlantic. Surely it would have been prudent to prepare for it: to have a remedy ready in the form of an effective emigration scheme? But, no. It was met by the usual far-from-exciting mixture of words and statistics. Nothing more.

The slump ultimately encompassed most of the world, and a bold policy concerning emigration would have been powerless to contain it. The distribution of people was not at the root of the trouble: at its best, redistribution could only be a palliative. But if it had been easy to get away, there might have been less suffering. Australia for example, showed itself to be much more adept at overcoming the conditions than England. The losses there were shared out evenly among all classes of the community: wages were cut by twenty per cent, and interest rates were slashed. Indeed, during this period, the dominion managed to wipe out much of its external debt. The question which remains, however, is: would people have gone? Strong forces tie an Englishman to his home. Nowadays, unemployed men will remain in a depressed area – even though there may be an abundance of jobs in another part of the country. The only certain recruiting agents for emigration are eviction and famine. Thankfully, they have both been retired for a long time.

TIME CHART

1607 First British settlement in North America

1620 Pilgrim Fathers land in New England

1758 First quarantine law passed in America

1766 Thomas R. Malthus, author of *The Principle of Population*, born

1788 First settlers and convicts land at Botany Bay in New South Wales

1796 E. Gibbon Wakefield, propounder of the "systematic colonizer" theory, born

1799 Marine hospital for immigrants opened on Staten Island, New York

1816 Bad harvests, plus unemployment following the Napoleonic Wars, bring about large scale emigration for the first time

1820 Population of the British Isles reaches 16 million: people become concerned about "overcrowding"
Cape Town ceded to Britain. First major emigration to South Africa, when 6,000 settlers land at Algoa Bay

1823 First Passenger Act passed in an attempt to improve conditions in emigrant ships
Attempt to relieve the over-population of Ireland by providing assisted passages to Canada

1824 Canada Company formed to purchase tracts of Crown Land for settlement

1825 New Zealand Company formed to establish a colony

1829 E. Gibbon Wakefield expresses his views on colonization for the first time with the publication of *A Letter from Sydney*

1832 Grosse Isle quarantine station established in the St. Lawrence near Quebec

1834 New Poor Law passed: the workhouse system is introduced, and emigration receives a boost

1835 New Passenger Act passed, stipulating more space for steerage passengers on emigrant ships

1836 New South Wales closes its frontiers to convicts

1840 Cunard Company formed: regular steamship services introduced on the North Atlantic
Colonial Land and Emigration Commissioners appointed to take charge of emigration within the British Empire and to administer the Passenger Acts

1842 Revised Passenger Act passed, stipulating increased space on ship-board for emigrants, and banning cargoes which might endanger their health

1846 U.S. regulations insist that all ships entering New York harbour shall anchor off Staten Island for medical inspections

1847 Potato famine in Ireland, followed by a similar disaster in the Scottish Highlands, brings dramatic increase in emigration figures. Dr. William Duncan, the first doctor to be employed by the state in Britain, is appointed Medical Officer of Health for Liverpool

1851 Gold discovered in New South Wales

1853 The Society for Assisting Emigration from the Highlands and Islands dispatches its first shipment of emigrants – from Skye to Melbourne

1855 United States introduces new regulations concerning food and space on emigrant ships – with harsh penalties for offending captains
New and much more demanding Passenger Act passed in Britain. Deaths on emigrant ships are dramatically reduced

1867 Shipments of convicts to Australia cease

1870 Poor Law sanctions emigration of pauper children

1885 Gold discovered in Transvaal

1886 By now, there are more than sixty societies in the UK providing assistance for intending emigrants
Statue of Liberty erected on the approach to New York harbour as a gift from France

1892 New York immigration centre moved from Staten Island to Ellis Island

1899 Gold discovered in the Klondyke

1911 R.M.S. *Olympic* comes into service, and provides steerage passengers with cabin accommodation for the first time
Royal Commission appointed to study the self-governing dominions as a market for emigrants

1914 Outbreak of First World War halts emigration

1918 The Royal Commission of 1911 publishes its report: recommends the setting up of a Central Emigration Authority to control emigration from Britain. A Bill, based on the report, is presented to Parliament – and rejected

1919–1922 Postwar emigration boom. Ex-service men and ex-service women receive assistance to emigrate to the dominions

1921 Meeting of Commonwealth Prime Ministers in London
First of the United States "Quota Acts," curbing immigration, passed

1922 Empire Settlement Act passed "to promote the development of Empire production and consequently of Empire trade." Training and assisted passages to the dominions are provided for emigrants: the cost to be split 50–50 between the home and overseas governments. In its first year, 6,992 people take advantage of the Act

1924 Second United States "Quota Act" passed

1926 Emigration under the Empire Settlement Act reaches its peak with 65,543 emigrants availing themselves of its help. Thereafter, the figure slowly declines

APPENDIX 1: EMIGRATION FROM U.K. 1815–1928

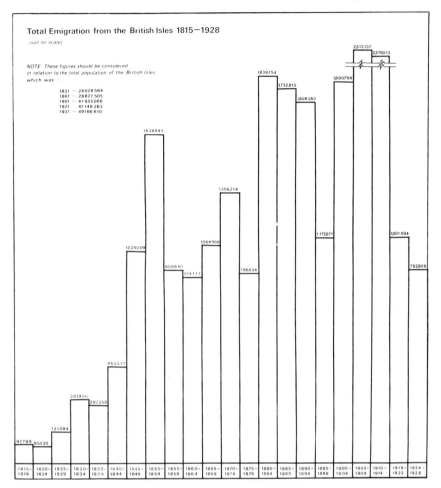

Total Emigration from the British Isles 1815–1928
(not to scale)

NOTE These figures should be considered
in relation to the total population of the British Isles
which was –

1831 — 24 028 564
1861 — 28 827 505
1901 — 41 855 066
1921 — 47 148 263
1931 — 49 166 610

APPENDIX 2: DESTINATIONS OF EMIGRANTS FROM U.K.

	Canada	U.S.A.	Australia/ New Zealand	S. Africa	Elsewhere
1821	12,995	4,958	320		384
1831	58,067	23,418	1,561		114
1841	38,164	45,017	32,625		2,786
1851	42,605	267,357	21,532		4,472
1861	12,707	49,764	23,738	no figures available	5,561
1871	32,671	198,843	12,227		8,694
1881	34,561	307,973	24,093	14,229	11,658
1891	33,752	252,016	19,957	10,686	18,132
1901	42,898	194,941	15,754	28,553	20,429
1911	213,361	250,969	81,294	34,528	43,273
1921	67,907	—	39,264	12,903	16,703
1928	54,709	—	33,689	7,095	13,489

BIBLIOGRAPHY

Terry Coleman, *Passage to America*, 1972.
John Maxtone-Graham, *The North Atlantic Run*, 1972.
John Prebble, *The Highland Clearances*, 1963.
Rowland Tappan Berthoff, *British Immigrants in Industrial America*, 1953.
John Hale, *Settlers*, 1950.
W. A. Carrothers, *Emigration From The British Isles*, 1929.
Edwin C. Guillet, *The Great Migration*, 1937.
Robert Louis Stevenson, *The Amateur Emigrant*, 1911.
Charles Dickens, *American Notes*, 1842.
William Cobbett, *The Emigrant's Guide*, 1829.

The author would like to thank the following for their help in the research for this book: The librarians of the London Library and the National Maritime Museum; staff at the Public Record Office; the Information Officers of the Canadian, Australian and New Zealand High Commissioners' Offices; the Information Officer at the South African Embassy; Mr. T. Greenwood, Secretary of the 1820 Memorial Settlers' Association of South Africa; Mr. John Dunn of the B.B.C., who mentioned the project on "The John Dunn Show" – and the many listeners who kindly sent in letters and other information. Without their help, this book would have been impossible.

Index

PICTURE CREDITS

The author and publishers thank the following for loaning pictures reproduced in this book: Mansell Collection, p. 9 (top), 10–11, 13 (top, bottom left), 14 (top), 18–19, 20 (top), 21, 26, 34, 36 (bottom), 39, 42, 46, 49, 55, 56 (top), 60, 70–2, 76 (top), 78–80, 88, 89 (top), 91 (top), 94, 96–7, 100, 104 (top), 105 (top), 106–7, 109, 111 (top, bottom left), 112; Radio Times Hulton Picture Library, p. 9 (bottom), 13 (right), 14 (bottom), 16, 24 (bottom), 25, 58–9, 61 (top), 62, 66–7, 103, 108, 110 (top), 111 (bottom right), 115–6; Mary Evans, p. 12, 24 (top), 28, 30, 36 (top), 45, 48, 61 (bottom), 65, 69, 77, 91 (bottom), 92, 98 (bottom); National Portrait Gallery, p. 15, 17, 20 (bottom); Australian News and Information Bureau, p. 47, 56 (bottom), 57, 86–7, 95; Public Archives of Canada, p. 63; National Galleries of Scotland, p. 73; Library of Congress, p. 74, 110 (bottom); Tate Gallery, p. 75; Museum of the City of New York, Byron Collection, p. 114; Canadian Pacific, p. 117 (top), 118–9; United Press International, p. 120–1. Jacket picture, *The Last of England* by Ford Madox Brown, courtesy of City Museum and Art Gallery, Birmingham. Other illustrations appearing in the book are the property of the Wayland Picture Library.